Will Macdonald

How to be a PUB GENIUS II

Will Macdonald

How to be a PUB GENIUS II

BACK BY POPULAR DEMAND

FIFTY more FANTASTIC TRICKS to amaze your friends

Virgin

MLFNWLFE

Praise be to:

Rod and Susan at Virgin Publishing, Scruffy Murphys, Callaghan's, Colin & Silas, Marcia, Louise, BL, Rory, Lewis, Finn, Yian, Archie H, Hugo, Elliot, Emilie, Emily, Georgiana, Albert, Fen, Jonny (again), Johnny (again), Sydney, Tim A, Ruth, Lisa W, Guy the Character, Burnside, Bunburys, Bilbao, B4N.

First published in this form in 1999 by
Ginger Books in association with
Virgin Publishing Limited
Thames Wharf Studios
Rainville Road
London
W6 9HT

ISBN 0 7535 0349 2

A catalogue record for this book is available
from the British Library.

Designed by DRi Design, Bath.

Printed and bound in Great Britain by The Bath Press, Bath.

Contents

Foreword

Hello.

Ever since being cruelly locked in an attic for three years as a small child with nothing but a barrel of beer and a box of matches to keep me alive, I have developed a small but slightly wayward skill for pub tricks.

It is only in this second edition of my published pub memoirs that I can truly reveal for the first time the inner secrets of how to become a pub genius.

I would love to share more details here of how to enter the inner pub snug of the mind, but I can't cos I'm off down the pub proper. No seriously, I am. No really. Honestly. It's 1.15pm on 21 July and it's my mate Brad's thirtieth so I've got to go to The Crown in Brewer Street. If you don't believe me, come down and see for yourself - although we may have moved on by the time you get here - I'll leave a note behind the bar as to where we've gone.

If, while I'm gone, you try some of these tricks, good luck, have fun, look after them for me. In the highly unlikely event of any of them going wrong, adopt one of the following emergency procedures, which should reduce your scowling audience to a bunch of helpless hyenas. Maybe.

- Smile sweetly and flutter your eyelashes so they quickly forget the fool you have just made of yourself and remember the reason they loved you in the first place.
- Blurt out this joke: man goes into a pub and orders six shots of scotch, all of which he downs in one straight away. 'Blimey, you drank those quick,' says the barman. 'You would too if you had what I've got,' says the man. 'What have you got?' asks the barman. '50p,' replies the man.
- Run for it.

A Lemon Entry

All you need for this trick is a nice, soft, ripe lemon and a lovely, crisp, new £5 note which your friend has just produced from his wallet.

The Challenge here is ludicrously simple, clearly impossible and jaw-droppingly brilliant. Bet your friend the £5 that you make the whole note pass completely through the lemon without using a knife, corkscrew, skewer, elephant gun or any other implement. You won't tear open the lemon and it will be in one piece when you've finished.

Can't be done?

Well, here's how.

1 Fold over one corner of the fiver to make a sharp point.

2 Fold or roll the note tightly, maintaining your sharp point, until you have a kind of dart shape.

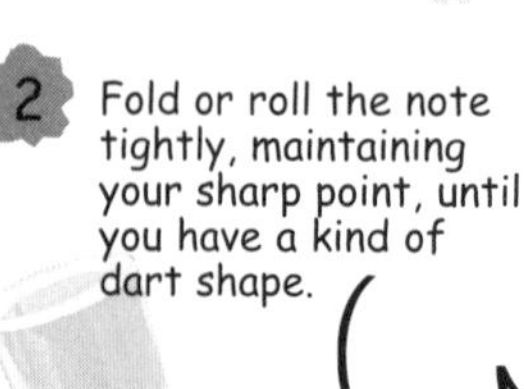

3 Now carefully push the point into the soft skin of the lemon. Feed the fiver into the lemon a little at a time.

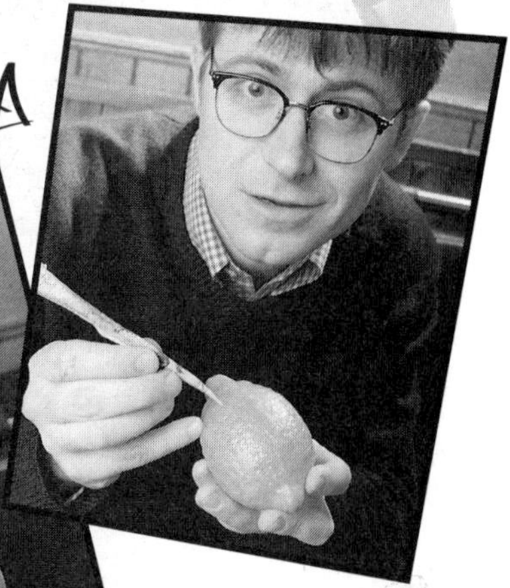

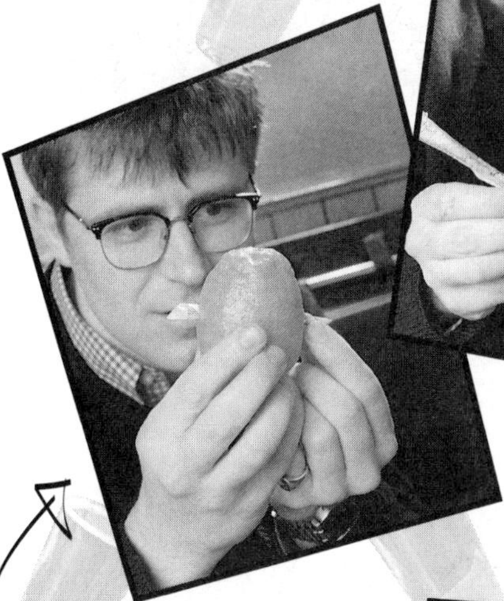

4 Eventually the point of the fiver will break through the skin on the other side of the lemon and . . .

5 . . . you can pull the whole note through.

6 You're left with a punctured lemon and a soggy fiver – but it's now your soggy fiver.

Waiter – the Dom Pérignon.

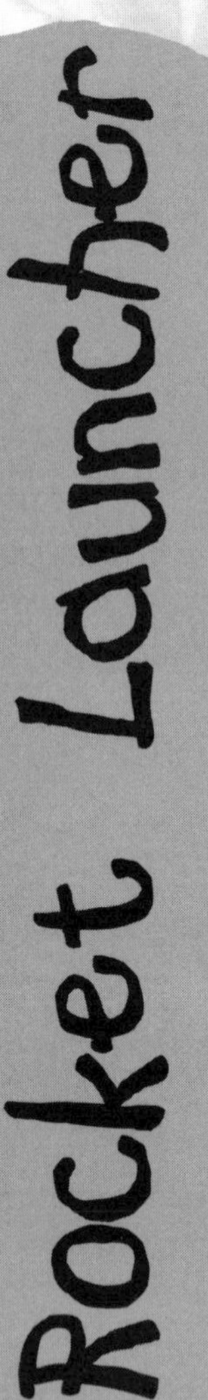

Spectacular, exciting, a real crowd pleaser . . . but enough about me, here's a trick to raise a few eyebrows – and maybe remove your own if you're not careful.

1 Take a freshly-empty vodka or rum bottle – either empty one yourself or grab one off the hopelessly strung-out wino lying outside the pub – and heat it up by running hot water on the outside. You'll also need a straw and a cocktail stick.

2 Now make yourself a teeny pub-sword by pushing the cocktail stick through the straw.

3 This sword will be your rocket (my son).

4 Next drop the rocket into the bottle and challenge everyone to remove the straw without touching it, the cocktail stick or the bottle. Obviously you will dismiss tipping the table over and other such pathetic stunts with well-deserved scorn.

Can't be done?

Oh, yes it can.

5 Light a match, stand by, and drop it into the bottle.

6 The rocket will shoot out of the bottle with a loud pop and a hint of scary blue flame as the remnant alcohol fumes ignite.

TIP: Make sure the bottle is well warmed to help release the vodka or rum fumes, otherwise the only thing which will happen is that you'll look a bit of a git.

Half pint hat trick

1 You're going to need a half pint and a small plate or saucer for this trick, preferably a plate or saucer with a flat surface and somebody else's beer in case you lose it all because . .

2 . . . the first thing you have to do is turn the half pint upside-down on the saucer.

3 Now here's the challenge – how do you drink the half pint using only one hand?

Can't be done?

Allow your friends a few desperate damp attempts at it before...

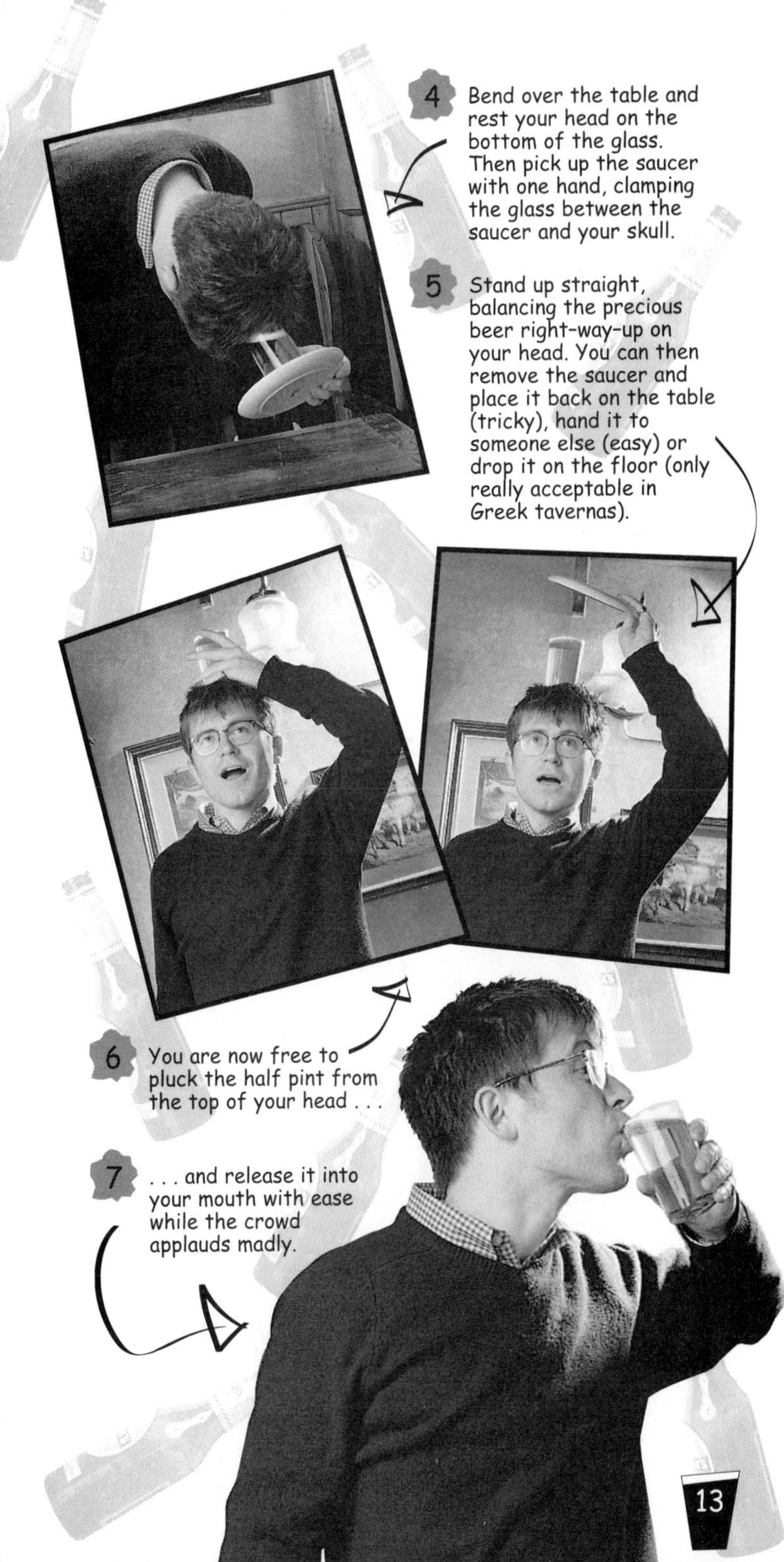

4 Bend over the table and rest your head on the bottom of the glass. Then pick up the saucer with one hand, clamping the glass between the saucer and your skull.

5 Stand up straight, balancing the precious beer right-way-up on your head. You can then remove the saucer and place it back on the table (tricky), hand it to someone else (easy) or drop it on the floor (only really acceptable in Greek tavernas).

6 You are now free to pluck the half pint from the top of your head . . .

7 . . . and release it into your mouth with ease while the crowd applauds madly.

Sherry Blower

A trick named after the Prime Minister's wife, if you say it the right way and . . . oh, never mind.

1 Place two large sherry glasses side by side and put an ordinary egg in one of the glasses. The egg should be placed narrow end down. Now bet your victim a glass of sherry – OK make it a pint of lager – that you can get the egg from one glass into the other without touching the egg or touching or moving either of the glasses.

Can't be done?

Would I let you down?

2 All you have to do is blow down into the glass containing the egg. Aim between the egg and the rim of the glass.

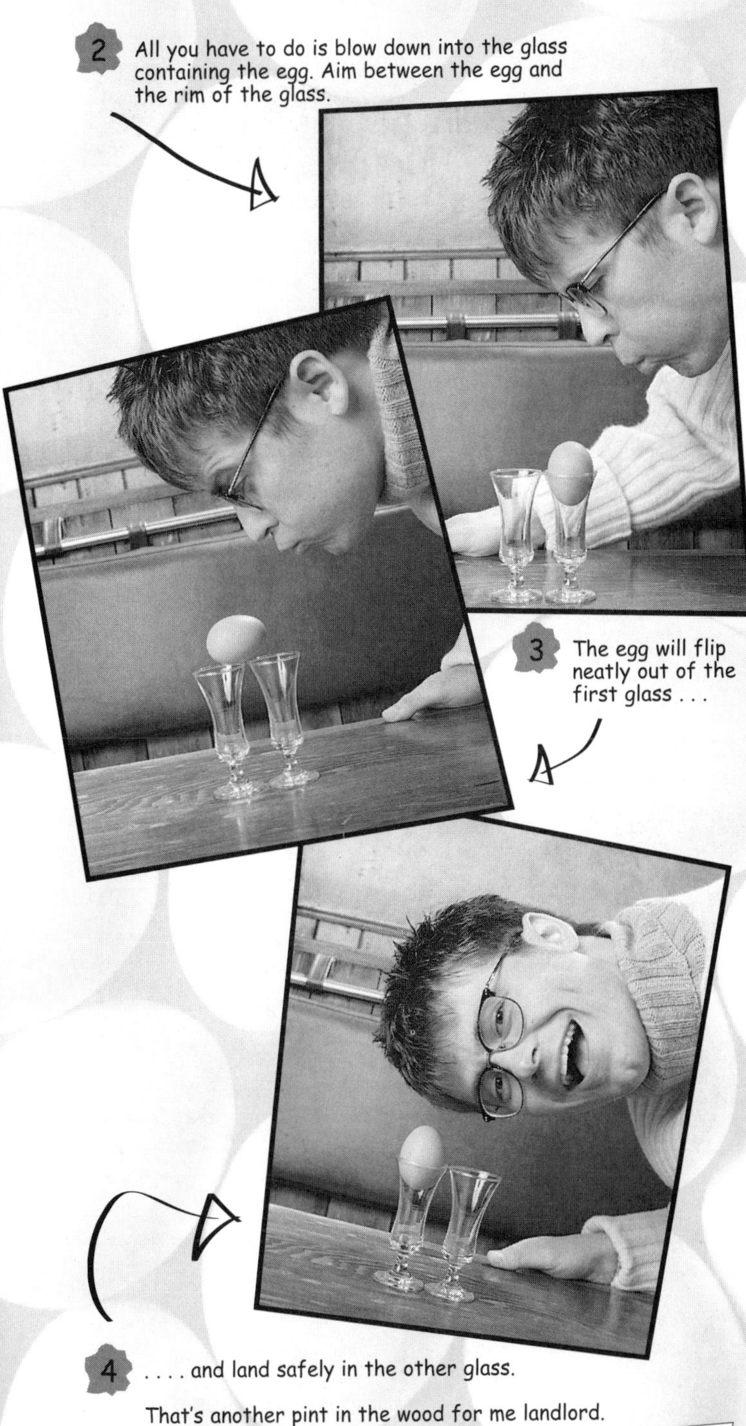

3 The egg will flip neatly out of the first glass . . .

4 . . . . and land safely in the other glass.

That's another pint in the wood for me landlord.

Soots You!

For this trick you need a gullible fool – sorry, good friend – who enjoys a good practical joke – i.e. he doesn't mind being made to look a total arse.

To prepare for this trick take an empty can (beer, Coke etc but not hairspray – no that wouldn't be a good idea) and gently heat its bottom with a lighter in secret. Give this can to your stooge and give yourself an identical untainted can. Now bet him he can't repeat your every move.

1 Open your can.

2 Take a drink. Maintain intense eye contact.

3 He opens his can.

4 He takes a drink. Don't lose eye contact with him.

5 Place your elbow mysteriously on the top of the can.

6
By now he's starting to think this is really easy . . .
7
Rub the can between your hands . . .
8
. . . then stroke your face in some bizarre ritual. Keep up the eye contact.
9
Not only does he think it's easy, he now thinks you've gone a bit nuts.
10
Run your fingers round and round on the bottom of the can . . .

11 . . . then drag your hand down your face. Don't break eye contact.

12 He will patiently follow suit, staring right back at you and . . .

13 . . . little suspecting that he has a layer of soot on the bottom of his can. Keep staring at him so that he doesn't look down at his black fingers.

14 Take another drink.

15 He will follow your lead.

16 Run the fingers of your other hand underneath the can . . .
17 . . . and wipe them down your face again. Keep up the intense eye contact.
18 He will go for the bottom of the can . . .
19 . . . and add to his new war paint.
20 Surely you can't keep a straight face any longer? He may have won a pint but he has lost face.

N-n-n-nineteen

If the Last of the Mohicans seems a little disgruntled at being made to disfigure himself in such an undignified way, offer him the chance to get his own back by winning a drink off you.

1 Bet Sooty a pint that you can make him say the number nineteen within the next minute. He's bound to take you up on it.

2 Ask him to think of a number between one and twenty and say it out loud. Obviously he's not going to choose nineteen, unless he's even dafter than you thought.

3 Now run through a sequence of asking him to double your number, say it out loud, add five and say it out loud until you get him to the number ninety.

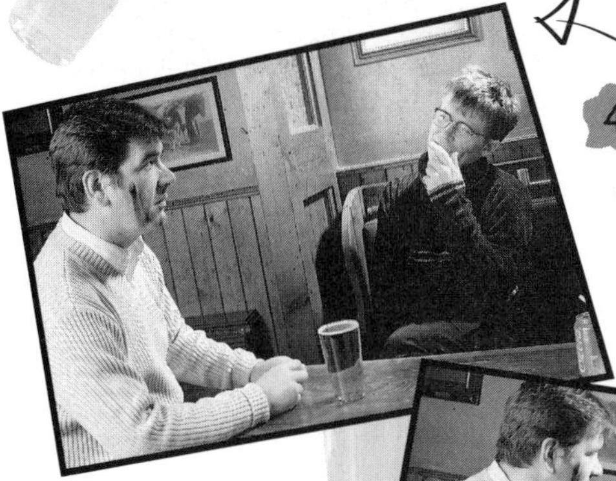

4 When he says, 'Ninety', you reach for the pint and declare – 'Aha! Told you!'

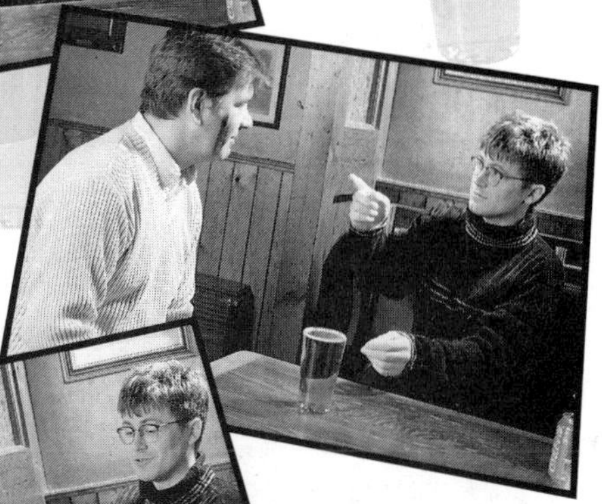

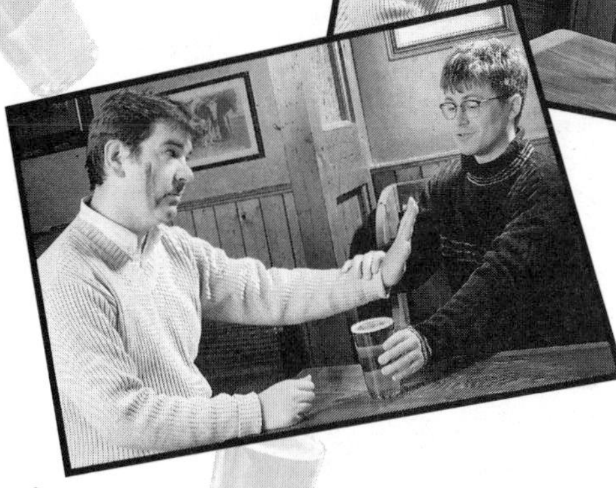

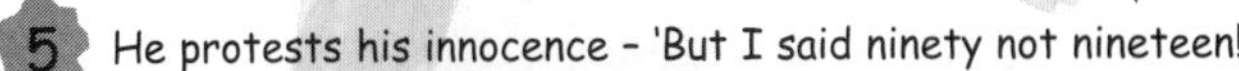

5 He protests his innocence – 'But I said ninety not nineteen!'

6 'Aha!' You suckered him, and the beer's yours.

FIVER BOTTLE SANDWICH

1 This is an impressive set-up. Borrow an unmangled new fiver from a friend, sandwich it between two bottles balanced upright, neck to neck, and bet him the fiver that you can get it out from between the bottles without overturning the top bottle and without touching either bottle.

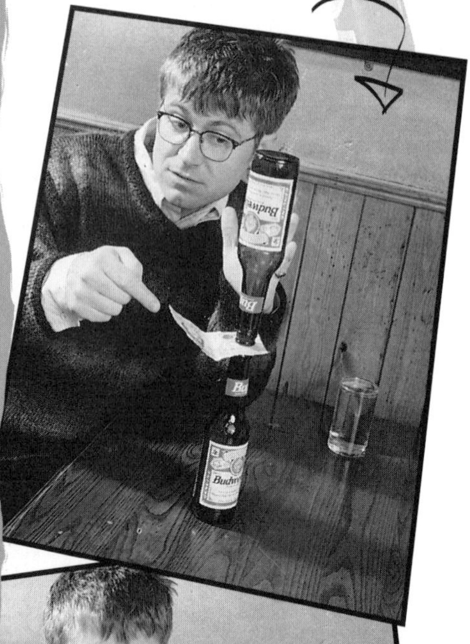

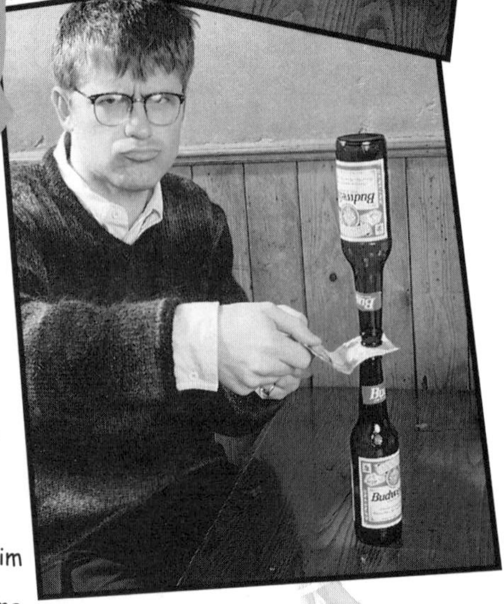

2 You can show him how impossible this is by tugging at the note. The top bottle will be very wobbly. Give him a go, watch him fail.

3 Once you've secured the bet, hold the fiver out straight with one hand . . .

4 . . . and karate chop down on it with the other.

5 A good clean chop will leave the bottles exactly as they are and you'll be five pounds richer.

Now do the decent thing and get a round in.

ONE GOOD TURN

This is an oldie but a goodie and works brilliantly when your victim has had a couple and left his thinking-head at the bar.

1 Set up three glasses in a row, the outside ones right-way-up and the middle one upside-down.

2 The challenge is to turn them all upside down in three moves, turning two glasses over with each move. To make it even easier for your victim, show him how it's done. If we take them to be labelled A, B and C from the left as you are looking at them, then you turn over B and C . . .

3 . . . followed by A and C . . .
4 . . . followed by B and C.
5 The glasses will now all be upside down. See - simple.
6 Now turn the middle one over and bet your drinking buddy he can't repeat the trick. He won't be able to do it, however many times he tries. Ever. Carry on betting, carry on winning.
Why? Well, you've given him the wrong set-up. The middle glass should be turned down at the start and the outer two the right way up. Look at the difference. Why I oughta...

The Side-splitter

This one's for the end of a session when the special powers of your drinking partners, Superman, Six Million Dollar Man and Xena, Warrior Princess, have been a little dampened by tequila.

1 Challenge them to split a burnt match in half length-wise without using a knife, enchanted dagger or laser-generating eyeballs.

Can't be done?

Pub Genius to the rescue. . .

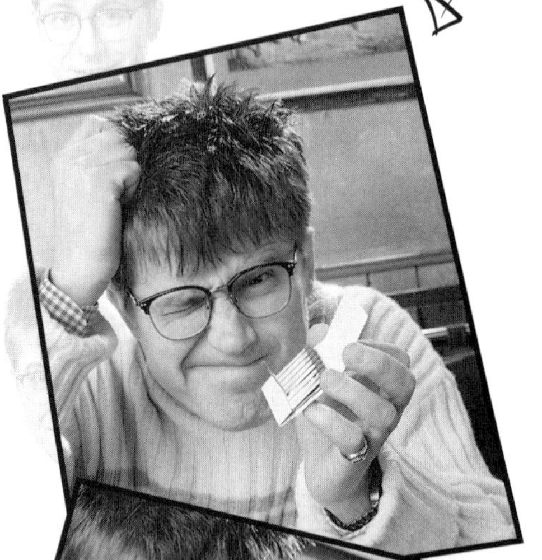

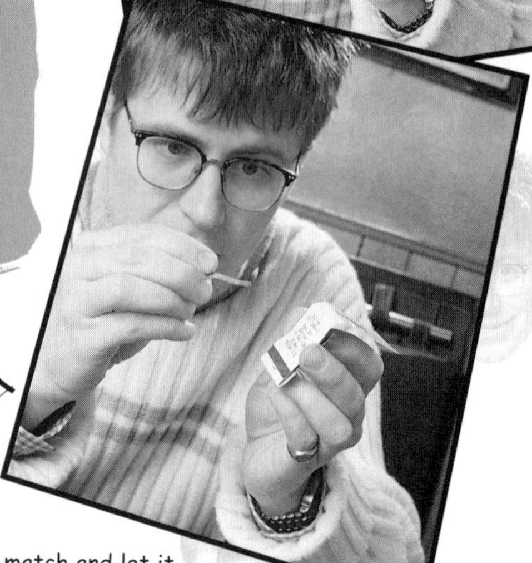

2 First light the match and let it burn right down.

3 If you clasp the match in the matchbook it should burn down without breaking.

4 Now lick the palm of your hand. (So <u>this</u> is the reason why your mum taught you to wash your hands after going to the loo!)

5 . . . and gently place the match on the tongue-lashed patch.

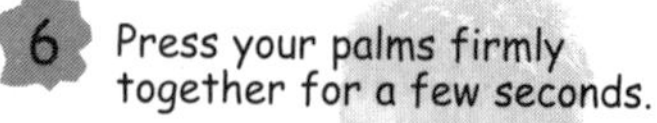

6 Press your palms firmly together for a few seconds.

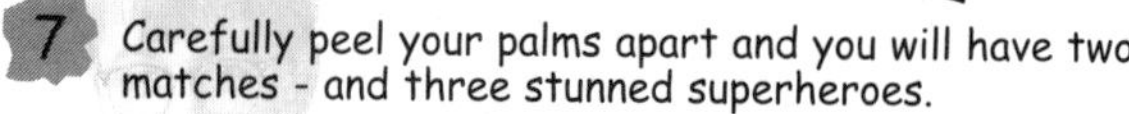

7 Carefully peel your palms apart and you will have two matches - and three stunned superheroes.

YOU GOTTA HAND IT TO HIM...

This trick requires the close and undivided attention of Mr Gullible again. Will he never learn?

1 Bet him that he can't count to ten as you do using three coins and ending up with all three coins on the table.

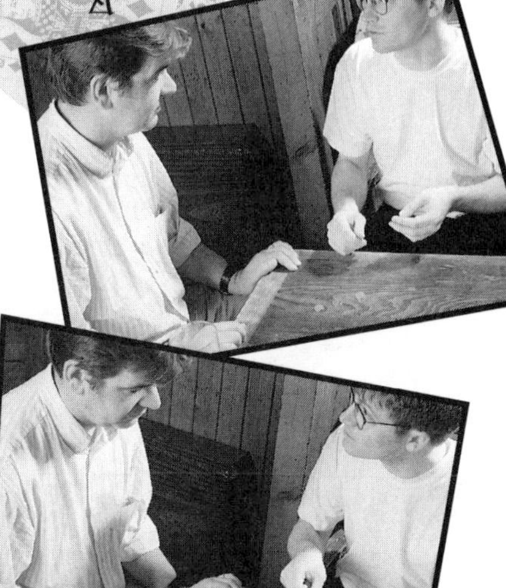

2 Lay the coins on the table and count them as you pick them up – 1,2,3 into your hand.

3 Then count 4,5,6 as you lay the coins back on the table.

4 Now count two coins back into your hand - 7,8 . . .

5 . . . and count them back onto the table - 9,10.

6 Pick up the coins, hand them to Mr G and ask him to count to ten.

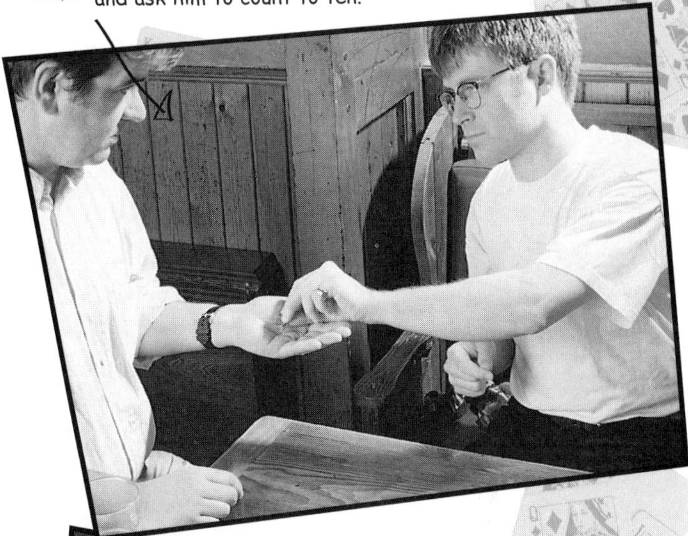

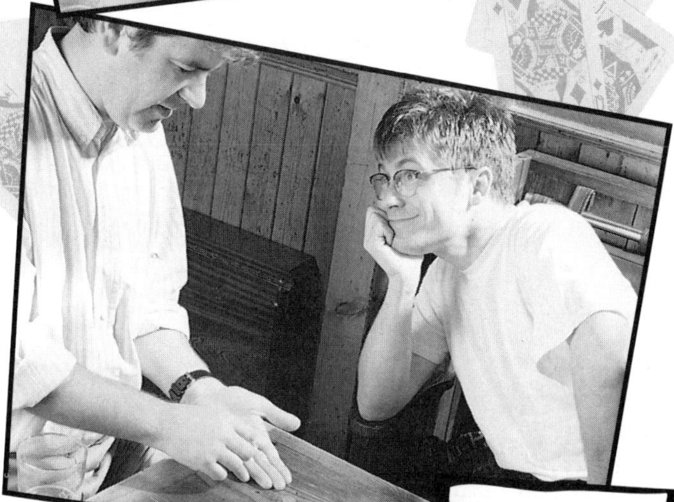

7 He will count out 1,2,3 onto the table, 4,5,6 back into his hand, 7,8 onto the table and 9,10 back into his hand. He may run through this sequence several times, but he'll never be able to leave the three coins on the table.

Why not? You have to start with all the coins on the table. Handing them to him encourages him to count from his hand to start off, and it's impossible to do it that way.

Clip Hanger

1 The question here is, how do you join these two paper clips together without touching them as you do so, using only a fiver?

2 The answer is cunningly simple. You have to fold the fiver into three sections, to form a zig-zag.

3 Attach one clip so it joins the back and middle flap.

4 Then you clip together the middle and front flaps with the other.

5 You must make sure that the clips are holding the outside flaps to the middle. This won't work if you've one or both clips holding all three sections of the note together.

6 Once you're sure you've set it all up like a real pro, just pull the fiver open. The paper clips will fly off, probably landing about three tables away in some poor sod's pint.

7 Fish the clips out of the unfortunate punter's lager and dangle them in front of your friends – they are joined.

Bottle Banker

1 You're down to your last fiver and you've just made friends with a coach party from Batley. It's your round. What do you do? Easy – put the fiver on the table and balance an empty beer bottle on top of it. Now bet everyone you can get the fiver out without touching the bottle or knocking it over.

2 If your chums try to whip the fiver out like the old tablecloth-from-under-the-crockery trick, the bottle is bound to fall over. What you have to do, when it is your turn, is roll up the fiver.

3 Once you have rolled up one end far enough for it to reach the neck of the bottle, keep going, gently nudging the bottle towards the open end of the note.

4 If you are very careful, little by little you will be able to push the bottle off the note.

5 The bottle stays upright, the fiver stays in your pocket and you stay seated – someone else is getting the £149 round in.

UNDER THE TABLE

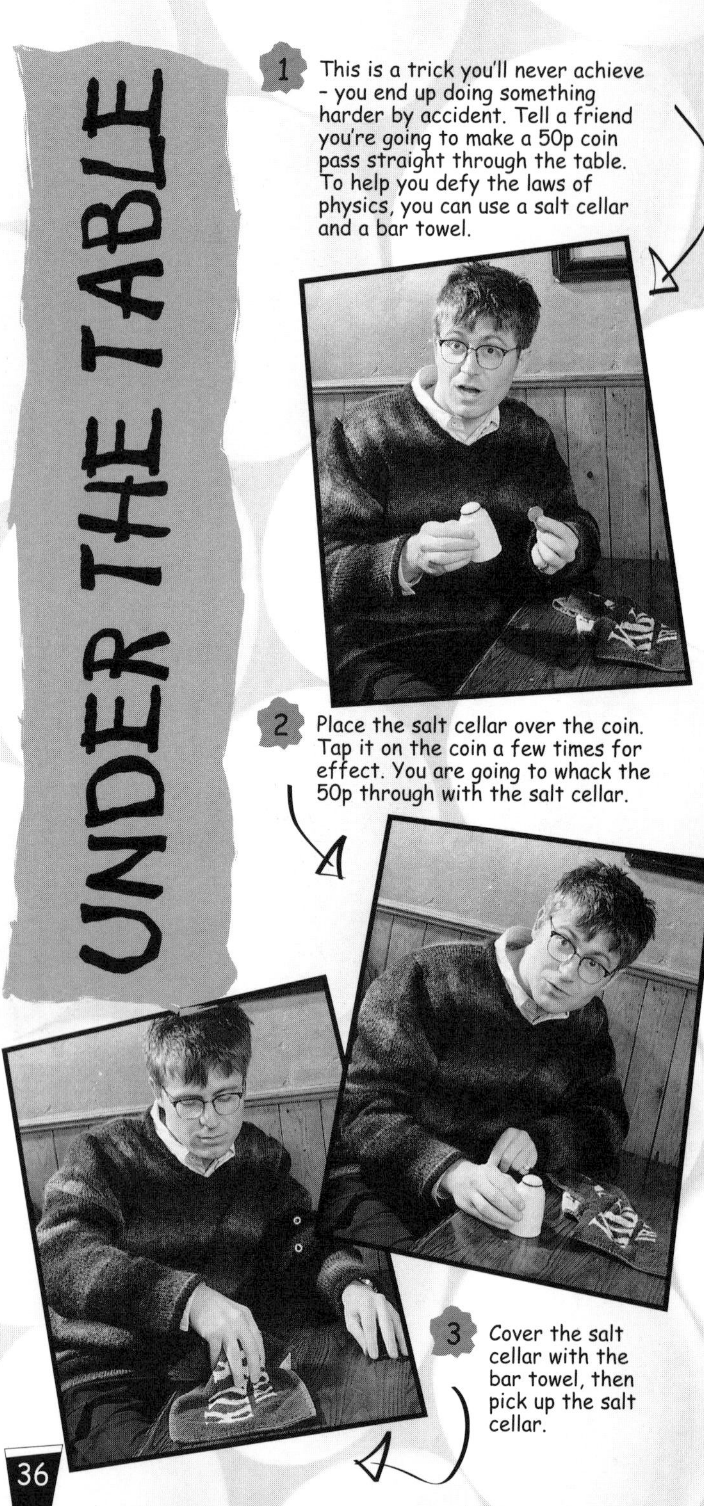

1 This is a trick you'll never achieve – you end up doing something harder by accident. Tell a friend you're going to make a 50p coin pass straight through the table. To help you defy the laws of physics, you can use a salt cellar and a bar towel.

2 Place the salt cellar over the coin. Tap it on the coin a few times for effect. You are going to whack the 50p through with the salt cellar.

3 Cover the salt cellar with the bar towel, then pick up the salt cellar.

4 . . . and smash it down hard onto the 50p, with an audible clank.

5 Lift up the salt cellar and look under the towel. Oops. 50p is still on table.

6 Bash the salt cellar down again and lift it to find, to your horror, that the 50p has still not fallen through the table.

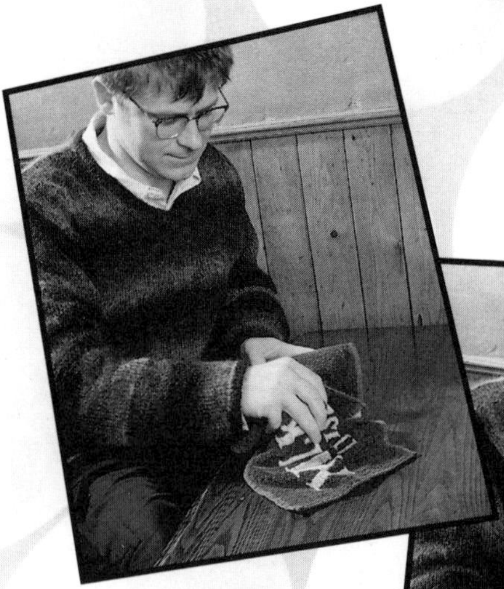

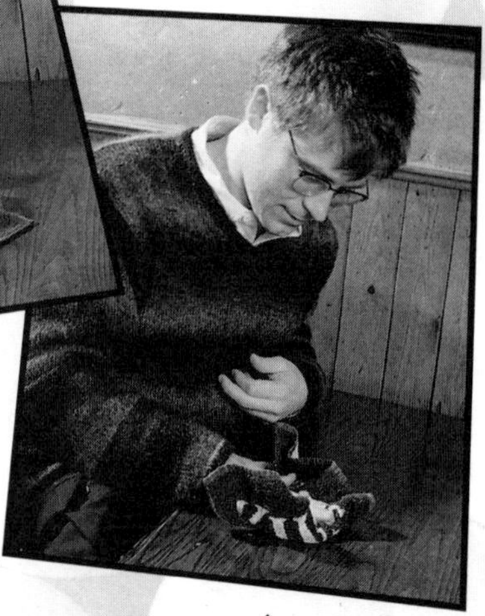

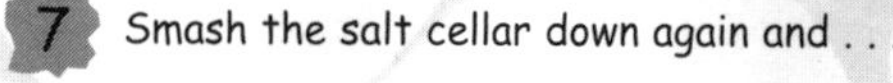

7 Smash the salt cellar down again and . . .

8 . . . drat, too hard.
The whole salt cellar has gone through.

9 So how's it done? Well, the trick is to let the salt cellar drop into your lap the last time you pick it up. The way you are holding the bar towel will make it look like the salt cellar is still in there.

10 Then, when you smash it down for the last time, you flatten the cloth.

11 You act bewildered that the salt cellar can have disappeared without the 50p falling through.

12 Just don't let anyone see you sneakily dropping the thing into your lap, otherwise the trick that goes wrong will have done just that.

1 What could be softer and easier to pull apart than a paper napkin? Actually, a napkin can be a lot stronger than you'd think.

2 If you roll it up quite tight . . .

3 . . . you'll find that it's not too easy to pull it apart.

4 You can pull till you're purple in the face.

5 You can pull till you feel your hernia pop, your teeth snap, and your brains fly out your ears, but you still won't pull the napkin apart. Challenge someone else to have a go and then bet them that you can do it.

6 How? Secretly splash a few drops of beer or water in the middle of the napkin and let it soak into the paper.

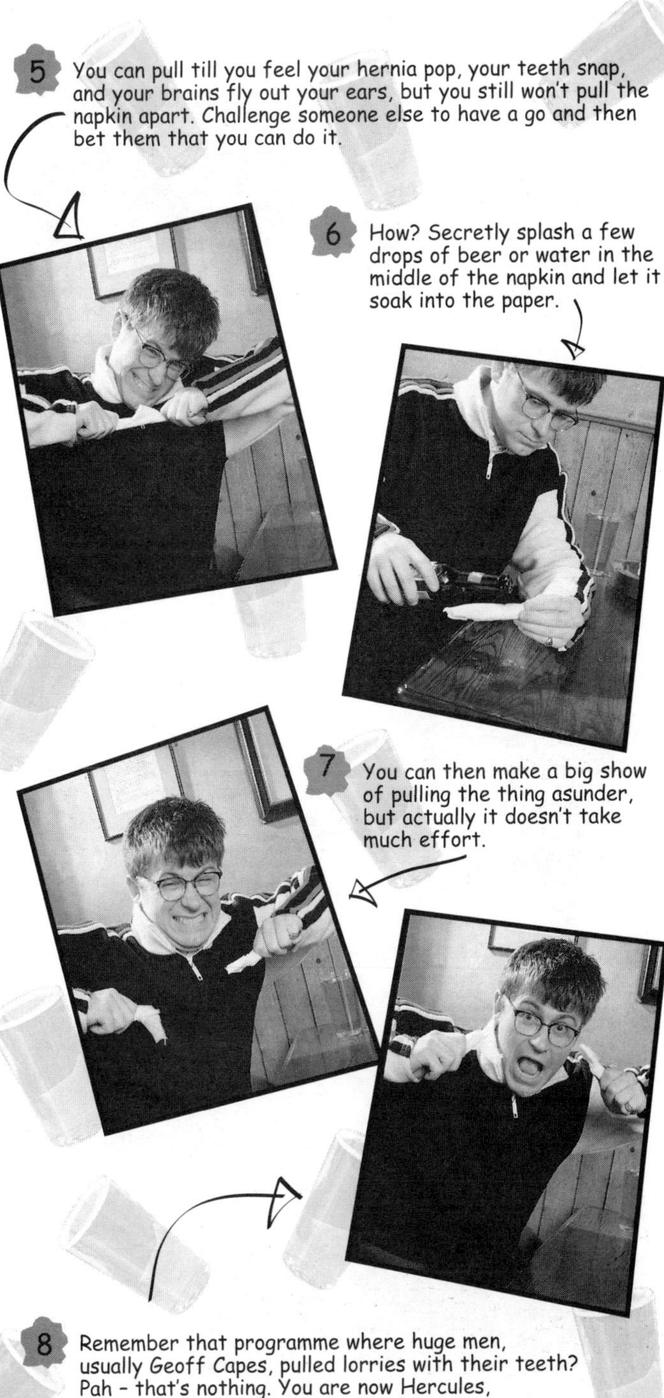

7 You can then make a big show of pulling the thing asunder, but actually it doesn't take much effort.

8 Remember that programme where huge men, usually Geoff Capes, pulled lorries with their teeth? Pah – that's nothing. You are now Hercules, Zeus and Popeye. Without having to eat spinach.

FORK LIFT BUCK

This trick looks impossible, even when you see it done. It's a balancing act that should never work – but it does.

1 In order to win a pound or two, or one of your American 'bucks' if you're reading this in Palm Springs, challenge a friend to balance two forks on the rim of a glass using only one match.

2 Following your friend's inevitable failure, arrange the forks so that the prongs sit neatly together with the handles facing outwards. Then you jam the match in, between the middle prongs, right up at the base. This should join the two forks together.

3 You now have a contraption that looks a bit like a seagull on a kid's painting. Sort of.

4 Carefully rest the match on the rim of the glass, with the forks to the outside.

5 Once you have adjusted it to find the exact balancing-point on the match, the whole lot will rest on the rim of the glass.

6 Another winner. Now if you want to look really flash, light the match that's overhanging inside the glass. Once burnt out it should really defy the laws of physics.

EYE OPENER

Everyone can control whether they have their eyes open or not, can't they? I mean, aside from narcolepsy and after drinking 16 bottles of Babycham. Here's how to prove that you can control your willing volunteer's eyelids.

1 Of course, there has to be a wager, so bet him a pint that, once his eyes are firmly closed, you can make him open them.

2 First, you say, 'Close your eyes.'

3 As soon as he does, you say, 'Not like that, you're doing it all wrong.'

4 He immediately opens his eyes and you've got him. . .

5 Easiest pint you ever earned.

Long & Short of it

This one seems crazy-go-nuts. Set up three shorts (of whisky, tequila or Domestos) and three half pints of beer and bet someone you can drink the halfs before they can finish the shorts. They will laugh like a drain and you can accept a very large bet.

1 The rules are very straightforward. This is a drinking race and you mustn't touch each other's glasses.

2 Ready? Set - GO!

3 He goes for his first short and starts to neck it with confidence. You are quickly on to your first half and gulp it back as quick as you can.

4 He slams his first empty down on the table with a smirk and reaches for No 2. You are almost finished, but lagging behind.

5 He lifts his second glass to his lips and starts to drink as you drain the last of your first half pint.

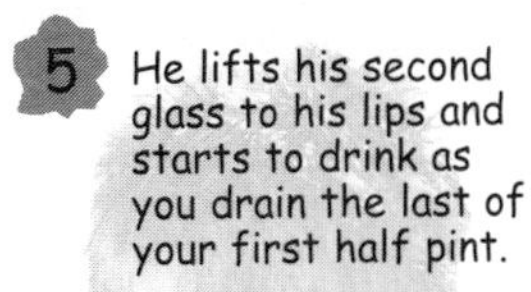

6 As he finishes his second, you reach across with your empty half pint glass and cover his remaining short with it.

7 He's not allowed to touch your glass, so he can't get at his last drink. All he can do is flap helplessly, then sit and watch as you enjoy the rest of your drinks, knowing that they haven't cost you a penny.

A JOB TO BLOW

This is a little strange-but-true trick which could win you a drink or two if you're in with a betting crowd. Why not try it at The Ladbroke Arms?

1 Take an ordinary paper napkin and an empty beer bottle.

2 Tear a strip off the napkin and roll the strip into a little paper ball.

3 Lay the bottle on its side and place the ball in the neck of the bottle.
Now, the challenge is to blow the paper ball into the bottle, without lifting or tipping the bottle.

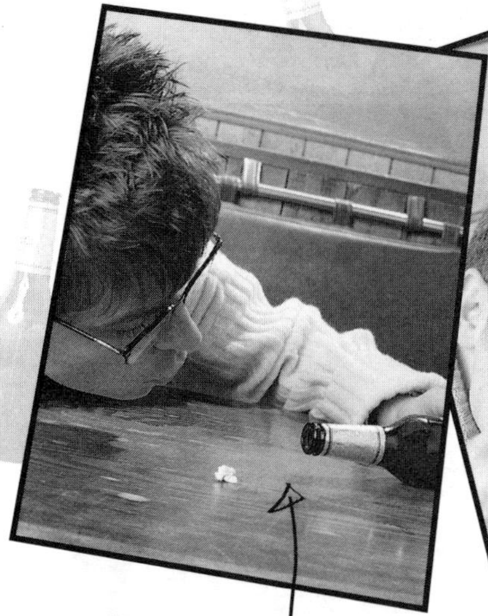

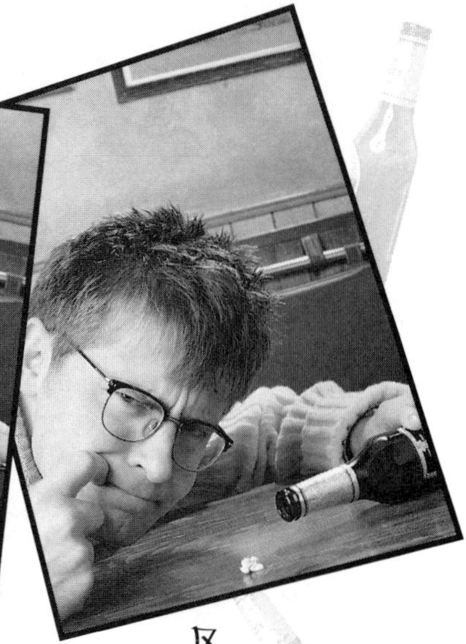

4 Seems easy enough. Most people will go for a straight, hard blow.

5 Unfortunately, this will make the ball shoot OUT of the neck of the bottle every time.

6 The answer is to blow steadily, slowly and gently, avoiding any backdraughts which will pop the paper out of the bottle.

7 Take it nice and easy and the paper will roll down into the bottle. Well I never. Who'd have thought it. Tuh!

1000 LINES

1 Don't worry this isn't an archaic punishment for ill-discipline, it's just a pub trick. The challenge is to write the number 1000 without lifting your pen off the paper and without joining the numbers. Try it – if you are to keep the '1' and the zeros quite separate, you have to lift your pen. Now wager a bottle of beer that you can do it without lifting the pen.

2 To do it without lifting the pen, you have to fold the top of the paper over.

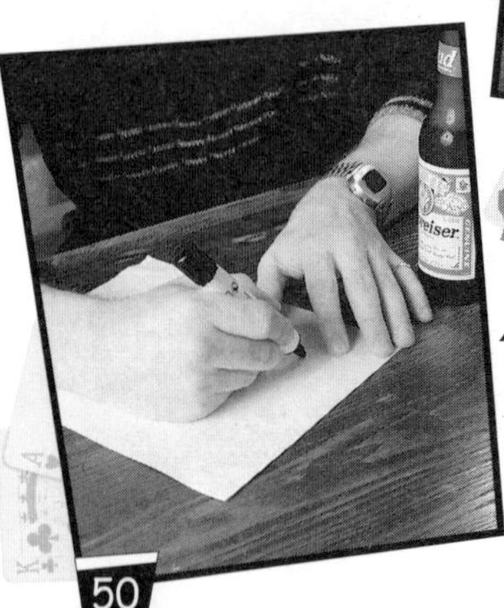

3 Start writing at the bottom of the '1' and let your pen run up onto the folded over part of the paper. Then bring your pen round in an arc, drawing a loop which will form your first zero. Let the pen run up onto the fold again at the top of the loop and bring it round for another loop to make the next zero.

4 Repeat the process until you have four loops.

5 Now lift the flap and, if you've been careful . . .

6 You will have 1000, written without lifting the pen from the paper.

7 You might also have won yourself a beer.

1 Wouldn't it be great if only we could read each other's minds? Wouldn't it be great to be able to simply feel what someone else is thinking? Wouldn't it be fantastic for bringing people closer together. Of course, we all have an innate psychic ability that can manifest itself from time to time if only we concentrate hard enough.

This load of old crap and similar bollocks should be practiced when you're alone, until it rolls off your tongue as though you really meant it. Only then will you be able to make your subject really listen and allow you to bet him a pint you can read their mind.

2 Take him back to his childhood. Ask him for names of roads, friends etc. Then ask your friend to concentrate on something that meant a lot to him, his first pet, maybe? A dog? Lovely. What was its name? Shadow? Great name. Keep thinking of Shadow. Tell me something about Shadow.

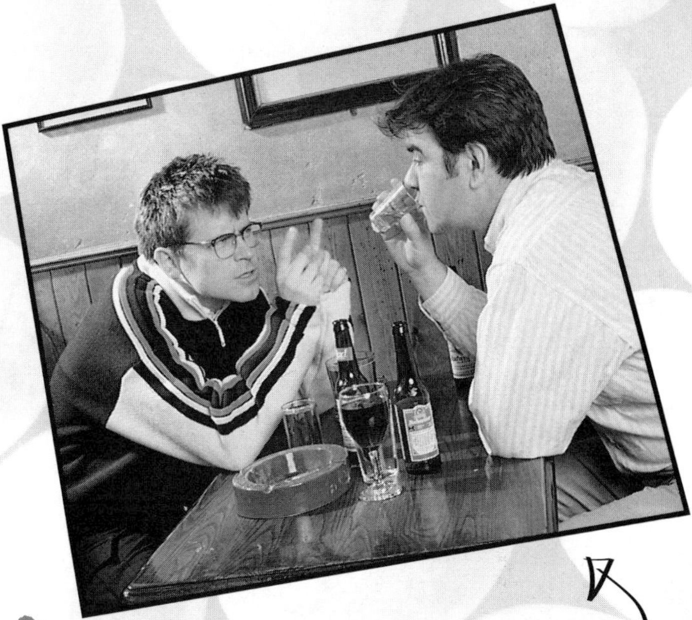

3 By now your friend either thinks you've had a few too many or that you've finally flipped, but he's going to be intrigued by your psychic experiment. Press him to concentrate, and yes . . . yes you can feel that something is happening. This could be interesting.

4 Keep the patter going, make him start believing that you think a psychic event is in the offing.

5 Don't crack. Encourage him to tell you more stories about Shadow (or whatever his pet's name was). Tell him he has to stay focused on the dog.

6 Oh, yes. You can definitely feel something happening. The Force is strong in this one. Now you both have to concentrate hard.

7 Stay focused, even when the barman comes round collecting the empties.

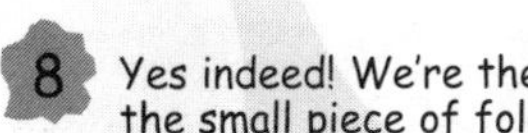

8 Yes indeed! We're there. Tell your friend to pick the small piece of folded paper out of the ashtray.

9 He unfolds it and, written in bold letters, is . . . SHADOW.

Of course, the barman is working with you on this one – he was lurking nearby collecting glasses, wrote on the slip of paper, scrunched it up and dropped it in the ashtray whilst picking up dead drinks from your table.

Only you and the barman know that, though.

Fists of Fun

Another night, another session, same old eejit sitting opposite you.

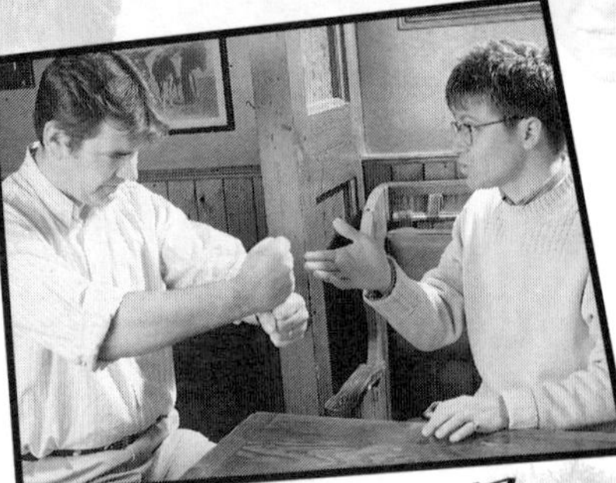

1 Ask him to make two fists and rest one on top of the other. Then bet him that however hard he tries, you can separate his fists with your weedy forefingers.

2 Bet accepted, crowd gathered, fists clenched, raise your fingers. . .

3 . . . and push his macho clenched fists apart . . .

4 . . . with very little effort.

5 Now challenge him to do the same to you. If you bet a pint he can't, you can be sure that he'll push very hard.

6 Then when your fists don't move, he'll push even harder.

7 He can push harder and harder until his ego bursts . . .

8 . . . he's not going to push your fists apart while your top fist is secretly clasping the thumb of the bottom one, giving you invisible finger glue.

The Final Straw

This is a brilliant drink-winner and it's unbelievably, footstampingly infuriating to be on the receiving end...

1 Lay out 15 matches on the table and challenge anyone to a head-to-head game.

2 The rules are that you have to pick up one, two or three matches each turn and you bet your opponent that he will always be left with the last match.

3 He takes up the challenge and picks up three matches.

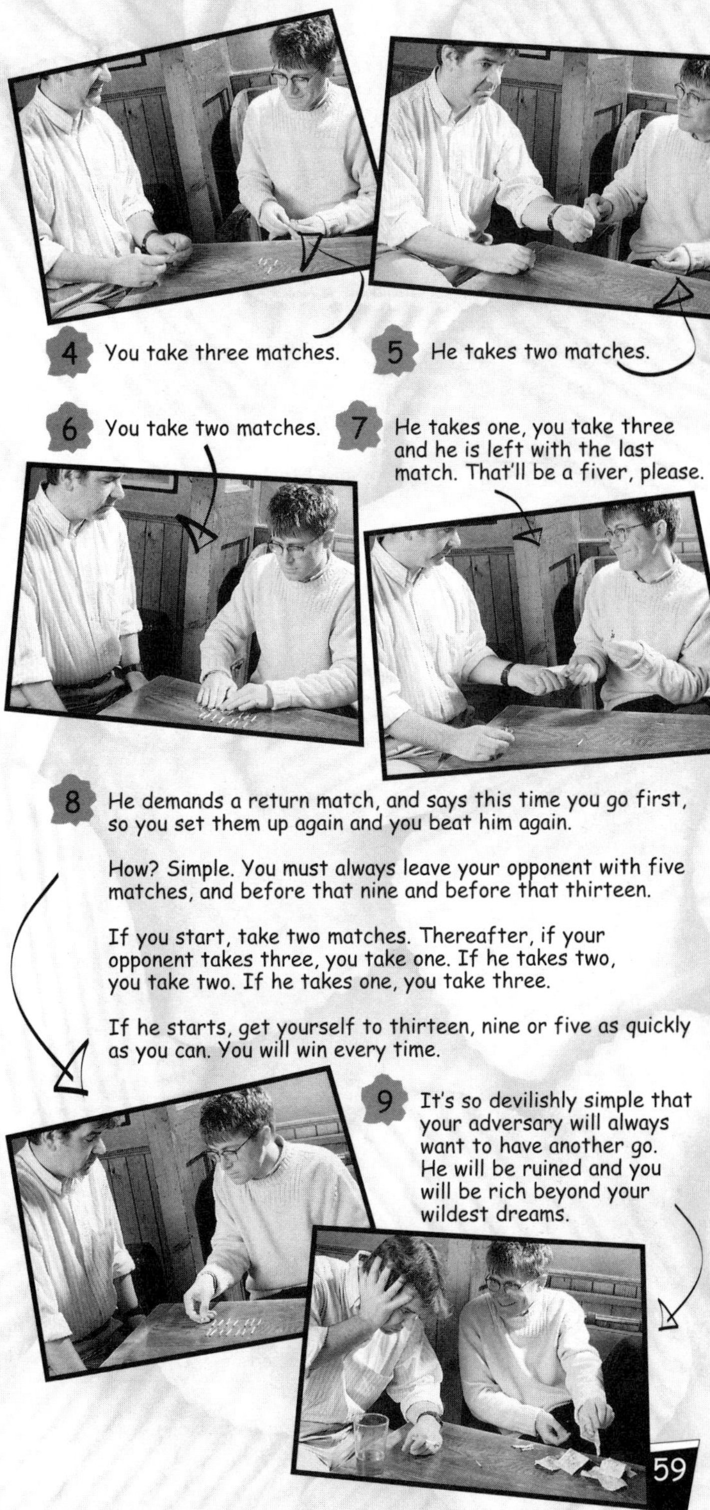

4 You take three matches.

5 He takes two matches.

6 You take two matches.

7 He takes one, you take three and he is left with the last match. That'll be a fiver, please.

8 He demands a return match, and says this time you go first, so you set them up again and you beat him again.

How? Simple. You must always leave your opponent with five matches, and before that nine and before that thirteen.

If you start, take two matches. Thereafter, if your opponent takes three, you take one. If he takes two, you take two. If he takes one, you take three.

If he starts, get yourself to thirteen, nine or five as quickly as you can. You will win every time.

9 It's so devilishly simple that your adversary will always want to have another go. He will be ruined and you will be rich beyond your wildest dreams.

The Loopy 2p

1 For this trick you are going to need a sheet of paper, a 5p coin and a 2p coin.

2 First, draw around the 5p coin . . . OK, so you need a pen as well as the paper, 5p and 2p.

3 Then, cut out a round hole the size of the 5p . . . all right, so you need a pair of scissors, too!

4 Folding the paper in half and cutting out a semi circle should help to give you a perfectly round 5p sized hole. Doesn't all this make memories of John Noakes or Leslie Judd come flooding back?

5 Now you're ready for the drink-winner. Bet someone they can't make a 2p fit through the hole without tearing the paper. Watch them rip your carefully built hole and grimly retrace steps 1–4.

6 Can't be done? No it would appear not, but wait . . .

7 Fold the paper in half again and place the 2p in the fold. Position the 2p over the 5p cut . . .

8 . . . then scrunch the edges of the paper together and the 2p will drop straight through.

SWEET KNOTTINGS

1 All you need for this trick is a piece of string. 'But how long is a piece of string?' I hear you all ask. Well, about this length will do.

2 The object is to tie a knot in the string without letting go of either end.

Can't be done? Not like this it can't. Watch as your friends attempt it and flail about like beetles on their backs. Collect your winnings and then take over.

3 First lay the string along the table and then fold your arms.
4 Pick up one end of the string in one hand . . .
5 . . . and one end in the other hand.
6 Then you just uncross your arms.
WARNING: Do not perform this trick too smugly – you may end up with your own arms knotted around your head.
7 Tada! - one knotted piece of string.

DRAUGHTY PILE

Draughty piles could be what you get by sitting in the boozer for too long with your back to the door, but in this case the draughty pile involves playing the draughts that have been sitting unused in a corner of the pub since old Jock and Jack McCoist wrestled each other to death after a heated game.

1 What you need is a pile of five draughts, with one of a different colour second-from-the-bottom. Now, how do you remove the coloured draught from the pile without touching any of the draughts in the pile, knocking the pile over, tipping the table, causing an earthquake, invoking the ghost of your long-dead Uncle Stan, etc etc?

Can't be done?

It can with a bit of crafty draughty... Firstly allow others to try, with the usual hilarious consequences.

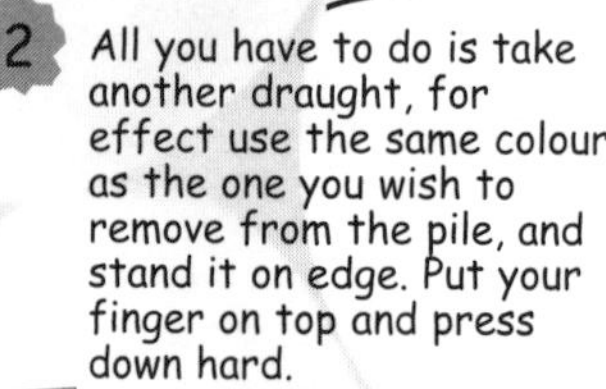

2 All you have to do is take another draught, for effect use the same colour as the one you wish to remove from the pile, and stand it on edge. Put your finger on top and press down hard.

3 The draught will shoot out from under your finger, travelling towards the pile at a speed previously only experienced by the crew of Voyager.

4 When it hits the pile it will knock the coloured draught straight out the other side of the pile.

5 Because that one draught has taken all the force of the impact, the pile should remain standing.

You may now applaud and those with bets to settle should see my accountant.

Backs to the Wall

You need a bit of space around you for this trick not least because, after a few pints of 'falling-down water', anyone you tempt into taking up this challenge will almost certainly end up doing just that – falling down.

1 Stand with your back to the wall and your heels together, your feet forming a 'V'. Place a pint on the floor in front of you. The challenge is to pick up the pint and drink it without moving your feet or bending your legs.

2 Sounds easy enough, but even those of you who, like me, have the balance, grace, poise, elegance and muscle tone (if not the arse) of an Olympic gymnast, won't be able to bend over without your bum hitting the wall.

3 Result – equivalent of severe drunken behaviour.

4 So how is it done? The technique is as follows. Clasp your hands together high above your head.

5 'Windmill' them round towards the floor like some demented keep-fit instructor from an early-1980s daytime TV show.

6 You should then be able to make contact with the pint without losing your balance.

7 Slide the glass up your leg until you are vertical again.

8 The feet are still in the starting position, but the glass is now in the drinking position.

9 Cheers!

Crab's Kicks

This is less of a trick and more of an amusement for young children and drinking partners who have, following an afternoon on the Malibu-and-Red-Bulls, reached the mental age of young children, but it should, nevertheless, form part of the repertoire of a true Pub Genius.

1 What you need is a paper napkin, a pen and a lime.

2 Draw a scary face on the napkin (and I mean scary. I mean scare the pants off them).

3 Twist each corner of the napkin inwards an inch.

4 Place the napkin over the lime.

5 Now give it a shove and it will waddle off across the table in a way that makes small children and big adults squeal with delight.

BOOZE 'N' ARROWS

For this trick you will need an ordinary piece of white card, but unless your local is equipped like the Blue Peter studio, you'll probably have to improvise by splitting open a beer mat – a strange but addictive habit in its own right.

1 Draw an arrow on the piece of card you have just created and prop it up against a glass. The question now is, how do you make this arrow face the other way without touching the card, turning it upside down, turning the table over, turning the room over, moving to Australia etc.?

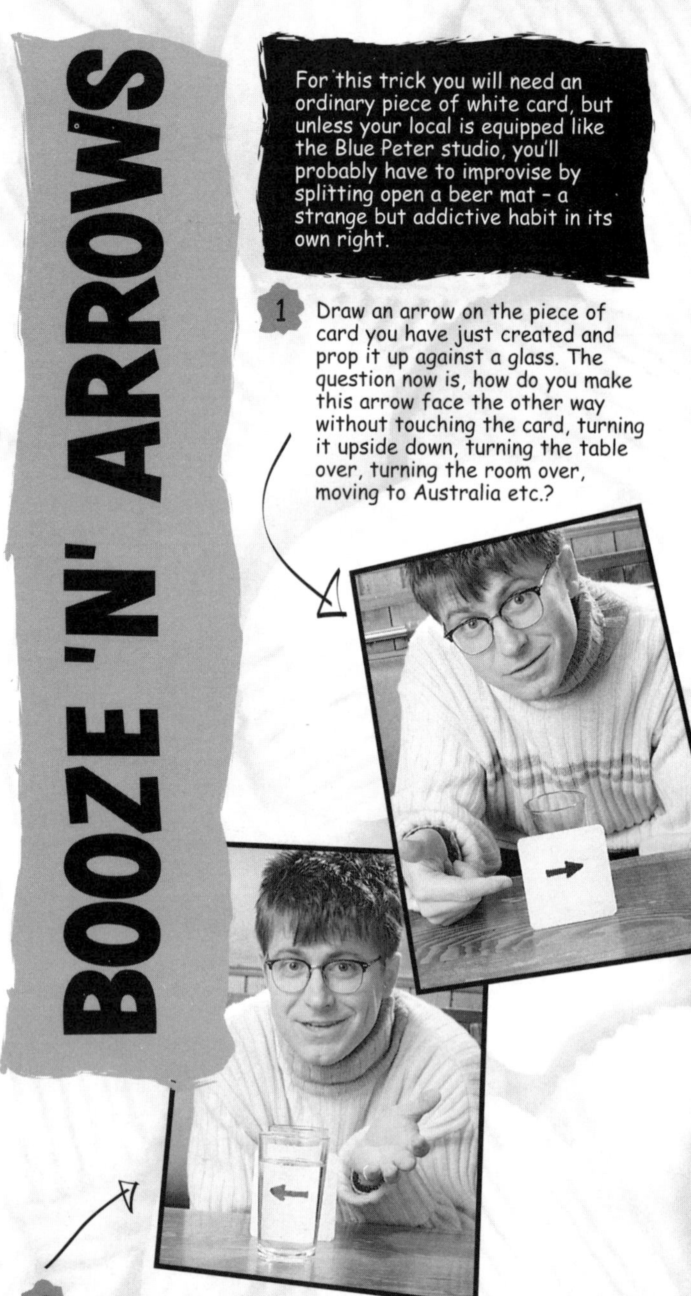

2 Allow your friends to flounder idiotically before revealing the answer. Place a glass of water in front of the card. Anyone looking at it will immediately see the arrow facing the other way!

Make it so that the arrow is now pointing towards the bar – a clear hint to anyone that it's their shout.

Card Be Done

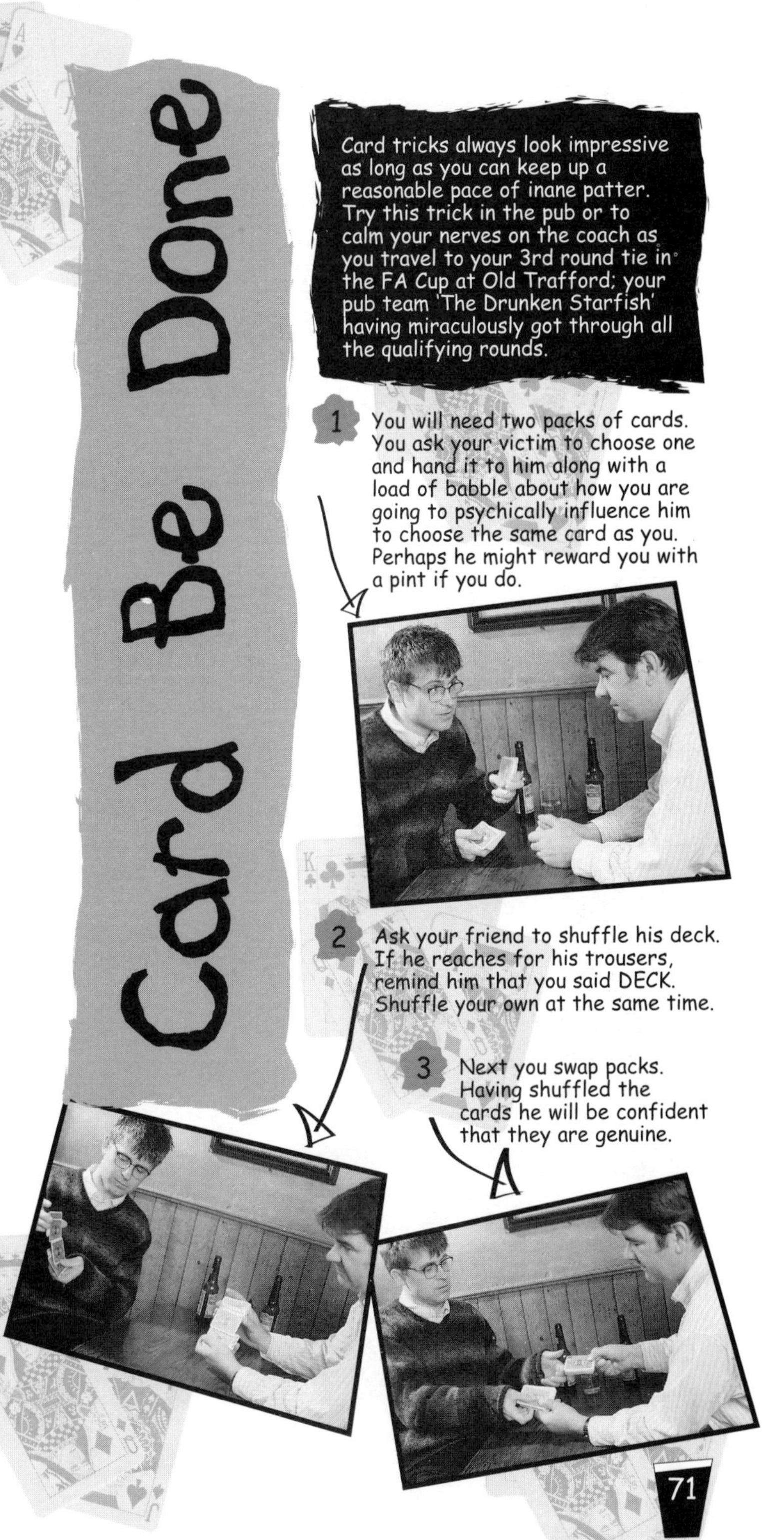

Card tricks always look impressive as long as you can keep up a reasonable pace of inane patter. Try this trick in the pub or to calm your nerves on the coach as you travel to your 3rd round tie in the FA Cup at Old Trafford; your pub team 'The Drunken Starfish' having miraculously got through all the qualifying rounds.

1 You will need two packs of cards. You ask your victim to choose one and hand it to him along with a load of babble about how you are going to psychically influence him to choose the same card as you. Perhaps he might reward you with a pint if you do.

2 Ask your friend to shuffle his deck. If he reaches for his trousers, remind him that you said DECK. Shuffle your own at the same time.

3 Next you swap packs. Having shuffled the cards he will be confident that they are genuine.

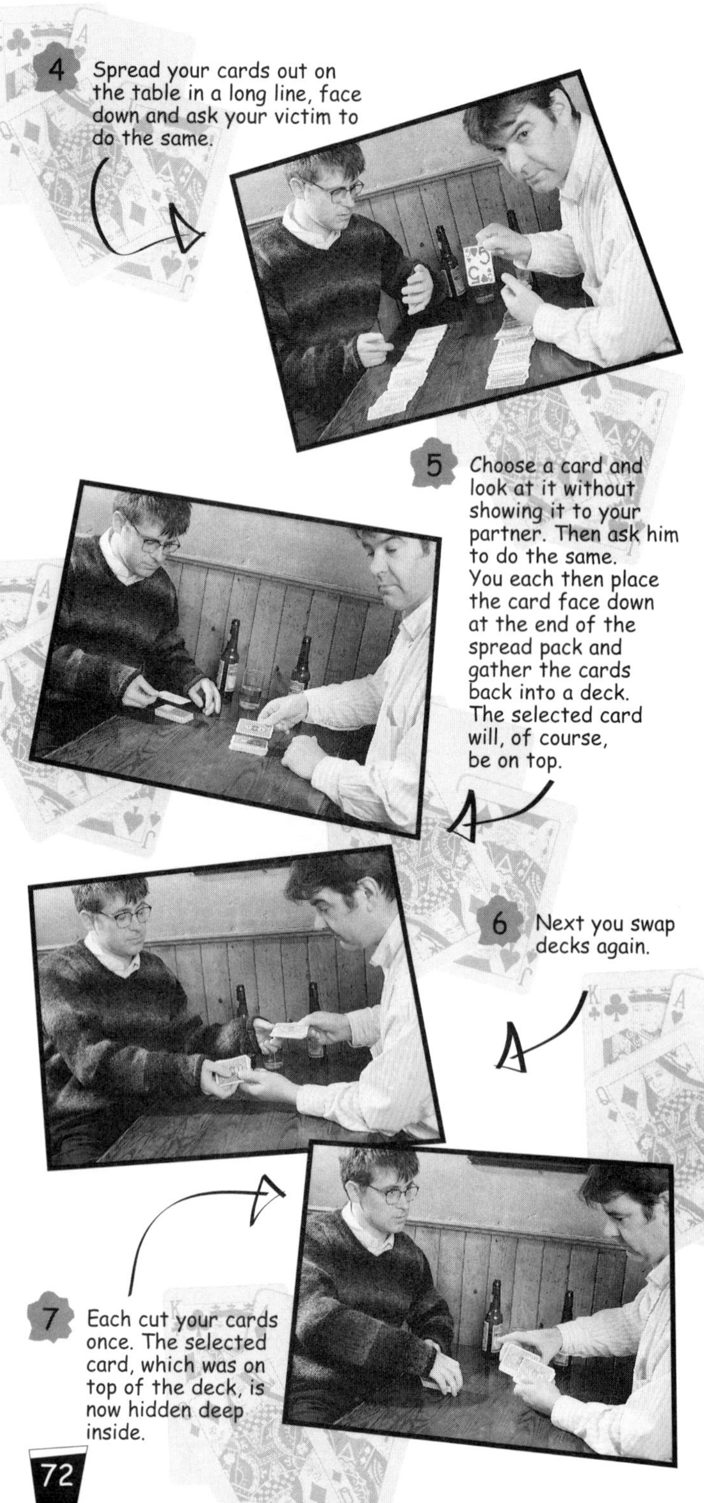

4 Spread your cards out on the table in a long line, face down and ask your victim to do the same.

5 Choose a card and look at it without showing it to your partner. Then ask him to do the same. You each then place the card face down at the end of the spread pack and gather the cards back into a deck. The selected card will, of course, be on top.

6 Next you swap decks again.

7 Each cut your cards once. The selected card, which was on top of the deck, is now hidden deep inside.

8 You now sift through the cards in your hand, pull one out and place it face down on the table, announcing that this is the card you chose.

9 Your victim now does likewise and reveals his card to you for the first time.

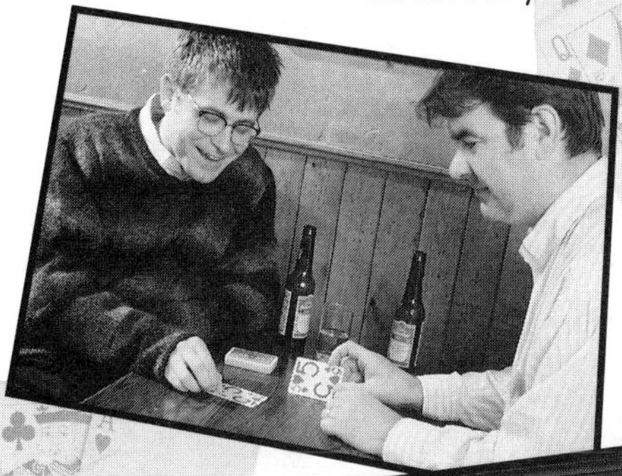

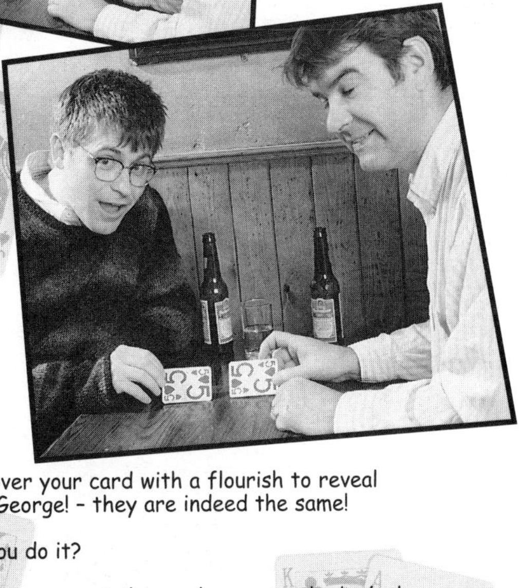

10 You turn over your card with a flourish to reveal that – by George! – they are indeed the same!

How did you do it?

Simple. When you cut the cards, you sneaked a look at the bottom card, so that when you put both halves of the deck together again, that bottom card was right next to the card your partner had selected. When you sifted through looking for the selected card, it was then easy to find.

A card trick with a difference, brought right up-to-date with modern technology in the shape of the ubiquitous mobile phone.*

1 Take a pack of cards and a convenient simpleton . . . er . . . friend.

2 Ask him to choose a card which he can show to you quite openly.

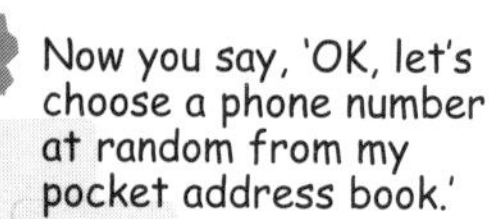

3 Now you say, 'OK, let's choose a phone number at random from my pocket address book.'

* Mobile phones are, in the author's opinion, the work of Satan.

4 Give him the number to dial on your, or his, mobile phone and tell him to ask for Paul when someone answers.

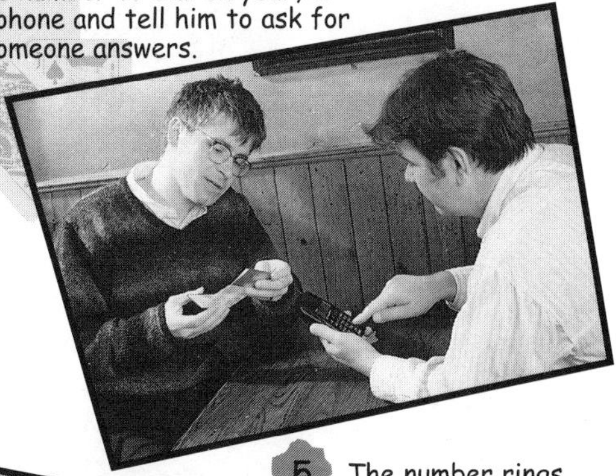

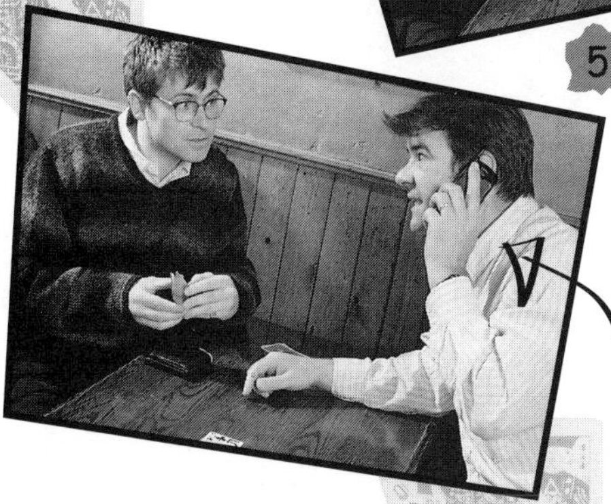

5 The number rings. When it's answered, he asks for Paul and then says, 'Will [obviously you change my name to your own name here, unless your name is Will, in which case . . . you get the picture] told me to ring this number and you would tell me which card I just picked.'

6 The response will be 'Five of Clubs', or whatever the card is that was picked.

How was it done? Well, when you looked in your address book, you will have consulted a list of 52 cards, each with a name next to it - e.g. 2 of Clubs is John, 3 of Clubs is Steve, 4 of Clubs is Tarquin (actually, try to avoid that one).

Find the right name then give your victim the telephone number of your accomplice who is at home waiting with an identical list to yours. Get your victim to ask for 'Paul' when your friend answers. Your friend, pretending to be Paul, then just has to look down his list to find the appropriate card. Bingo.

On Me Head Son

This one's profitable for you, yet painful and perplexing for your friend. Bet a (sturdy but non-violent) acquaintance that he can't remove a coin stuck to his forehead without touching it.

1 Warm him up by running through the trick yourself. Press a coin firmly onto your forehead.

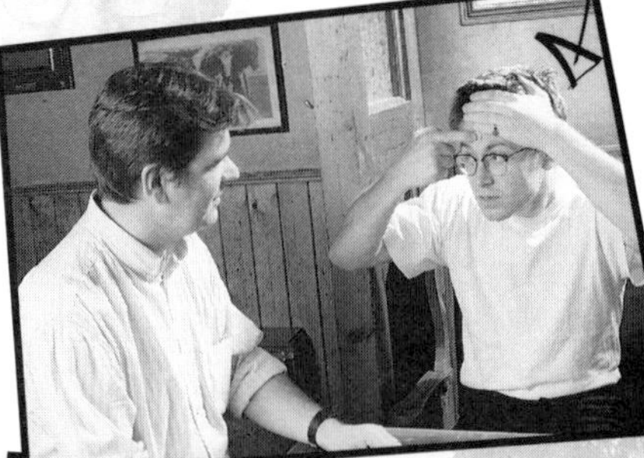

2 Unless you're some kind of alien, your skin is such that the coin will stick there. So how do you remove it without touching it?

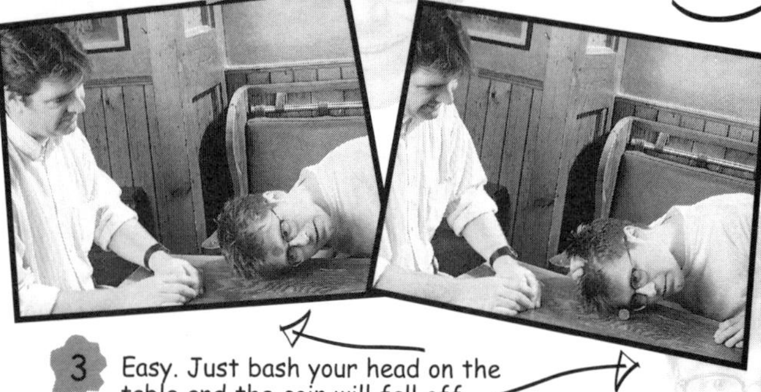

3 Easy. Just bash your head on the table and the coin will fall off.

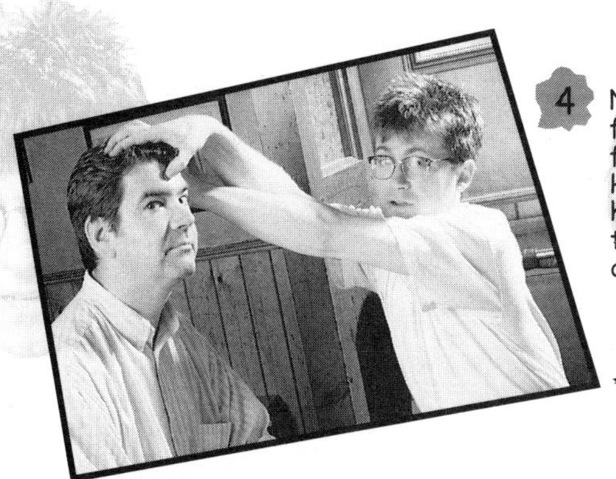

4 Now press the coin firmly onto you friend's forehead. He will then bash his head on the table trying to dislodge the coin.

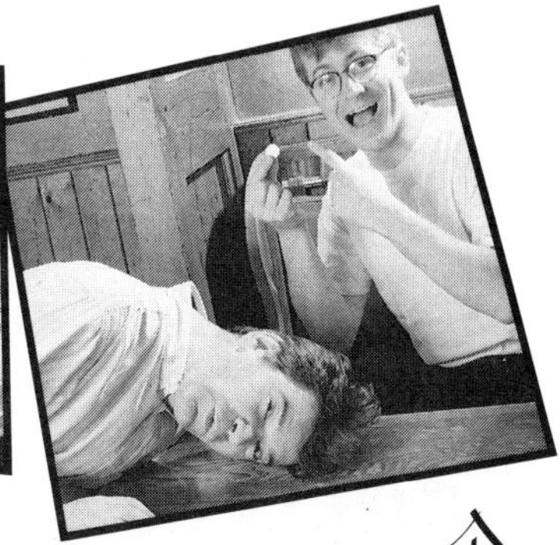

5 What he doesn't know is that, although you pressed the coin really hard against his forehead, you didn't leave it there. You plucked it off his skin as soon as you finished pressing. With you having pressed so hard, it will have felt like it was still there.

6 Make sure he sees the funny side when you tell him and don't let him bash his head on the table for too long, otherwise you might get your own head bashed in.

Warning: Don't try this on mates who are about to sit their finals.

THE POWER OF MONEY

1 For this trick you will need an ordinary wooden pencil, a five pound note and somebody daft enough to believe that you can break a solid pencil with a flimsy fiver.

2 Get the fool to hold out the pencil just as though you are about to perform a martial arts brick chopping demonstration.

3 Fold the note down the middle and tell your crony that it is with the resulting edge that you will snap the pencil. Take a generous backswing and slash the fiver down on the pencil.

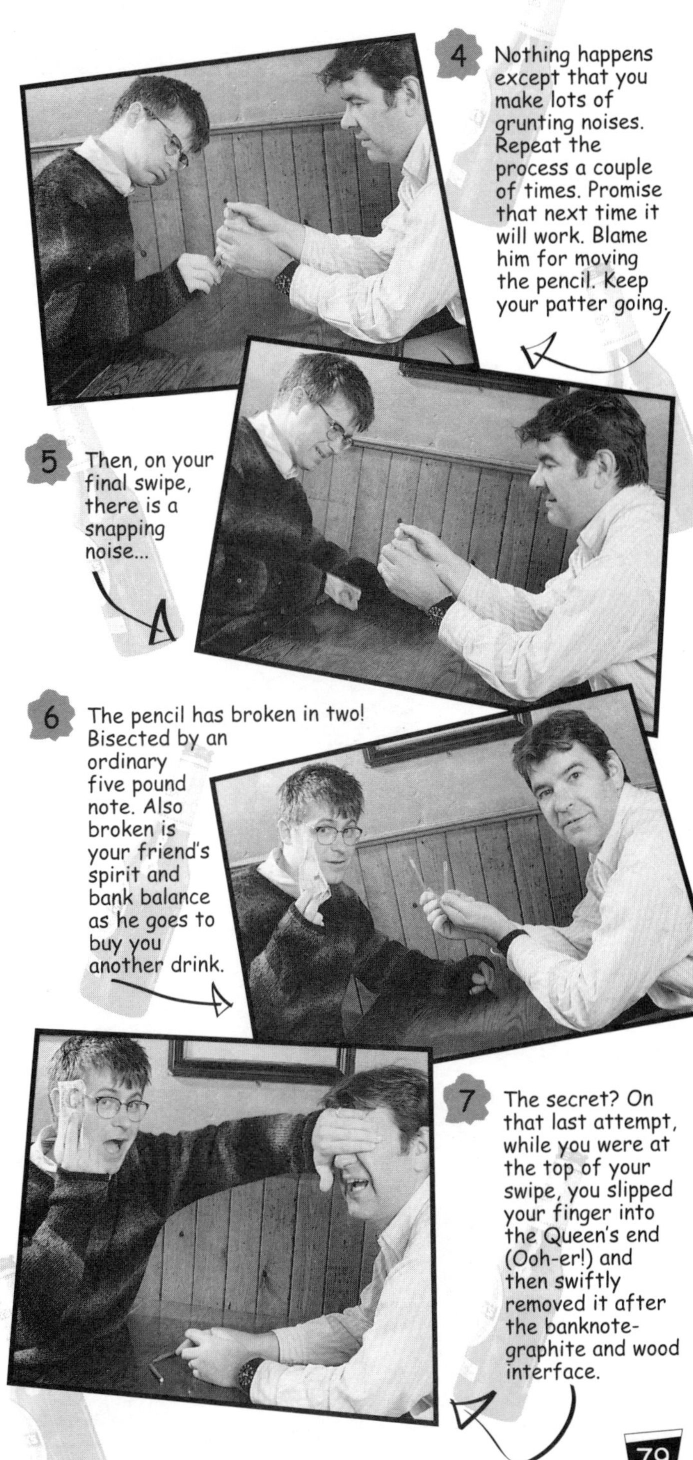

4 Nothing happens except that you make lots of grunting noises. Repeat the process a couple of times. Promise that next time it will work. Blame him for moving the pencil. Keep your patter going.

5 Then, on your final swipe, there is a snapping noise...

6 The pencil has broken in two! Bisected by an ordinary five pound note. Also broken is your friend's spirit and bank balance as he goes to buy you another drink.

7 The secret? On that last attempt, while you were at the top of your swipe, you slipped your finger into the Queen's end (Ooh-er!) and then swiftly removed it after the banknote-graphite and wood interface.

Creative Accountancy

This one could make you a pint millionaire in a few seconds. Bet as many pub-goers as you like they can't follow your simple instructions to the letter (or in this case, to the number). Why not do it on a quiz night when everyone has a pen and paper and you have a microphone?

1 Ask your victims to write down the number five hundred and ninety six.

2 They will write 596.

3 Ask them to write down one thousand, three hundred and twenty seven. They will write 1327.

4 Ask them to write down twelve thousand, twelve hundred and twelve.

5 They will write 121212. This, of course is one hundred and twenty one thousand, two hundred and twelve.

6 Twelve thousand, twelve hundred and twelve is actually 13212. Now simply collect all the winnings from your numerically-challenged friends.

RATTLE AND DUMB

This is a different spin on the old 'Find the lady' card trick or 'Which cup is the pea under?' trick. In the case of my less than astute colleague, it might as well have been 'Which matchbox is the table under?' The trick here is to guess which box contains the matches.

1 Show your friend the three matchboxes on the table, all open. Only one box contains matches. Close the boxes, pick up the one with the matches in it and give it a shake so that he can hear the rattle of the matches.

2 Now bet him a beer that he can't pick out that matchbox after you have mixed them up and re-arranged them on the table.

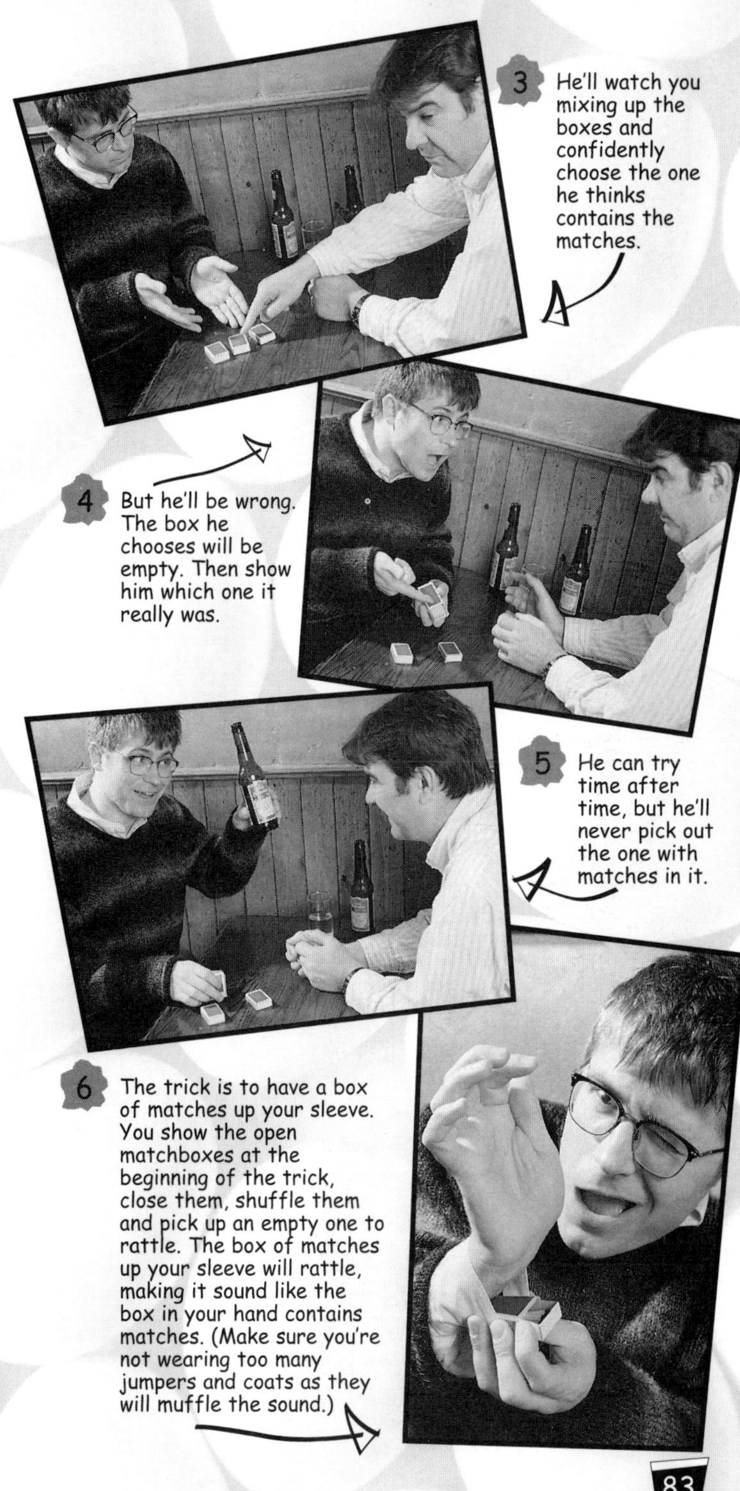

3 He'll watch you mixing up the boxes and confidently choose the one he thinks contains the matches.

4 But he'll be wrong. The box he chooses will be empty. Then show him which one it really was.

5 He can try time after time, but he'll never pick out the one with matches in it.

6 The trick is to have a box of matches up your sleeve. You show the open matchboxes at the beginning of the trick, close them, shuffle them and pick up an empty one to rattle. The box of matches up your sleeve will rattle, making it sound like the box in your hand contains matches. (Make sure you're not wearing too many jumpers and coats as they will muffle the sound.)

Half Past One

Without a doubt, the best pub tricks involve beer, drinking beer, winning beer, drinking beer, more beer and drinking beer, so here's a beer trick.*

1 Line up three lovely half pints full of beer alongside three sad little empty half pint glasses. Bet your friends a beer that you can re-arrange the glasses so that they line up alternatively full and empty by moving only one glass.

Can't be done?

Bored of that question yet?

2 Pick up the middle of the three half pints. Resist the overwhelming urge to down it in one.

*The author and publishers wish to point out that drinking beer is neither big nor clever. However, drinking neat gin and lighter fluid is.

3 Pour the beer into the middle glass of the three empty half pint glasses.

4 Replace the glass you picked up and the line-up of alternate full and empty glasses is complete, with you having only touched one glass.

Now drink the lot and demand some more.

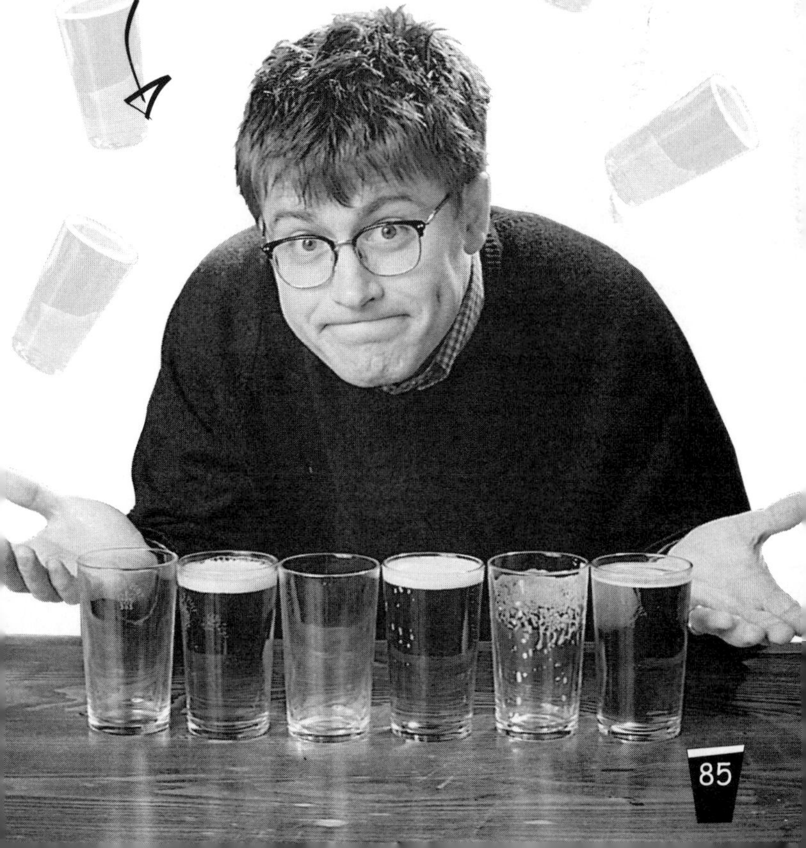

It's a Shocker

This trick is likely to elicit a good deal of scepticism, even from somebody who's had a few, so make sure you work on your patter – the fun of this thing is all in the build-up.

1 Take a matchbox and tuck a match down each side. Tell your friend that this is an incredible phenomenon – a matchbox like this can, under the right conditions, actually hold an electric charge as if it's been connected to the mains. The two matches are the positive and negative terminals and if he were to join the circuit he'd generate a major shock.

2 He won't believe you so remain stern and serious and ask him to lick the index finger of his right hand and touch one of the 'terminals' – but do it carefully!

3 Slowly, now. Don't make any sudden moves. He touches the terminal and nothing happens. No shock this time.

4 Now you ask him to lick the index finger on his left hand and touch the other 'terminal'.

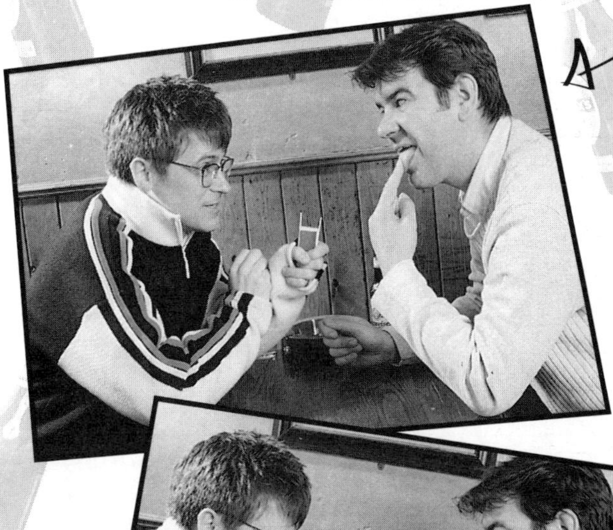

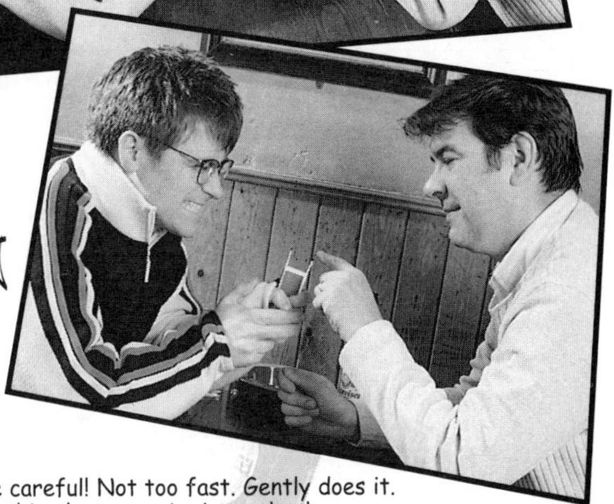

5 Be careful! Not too fast. Gently does it. Nothing happens. Again no shock.

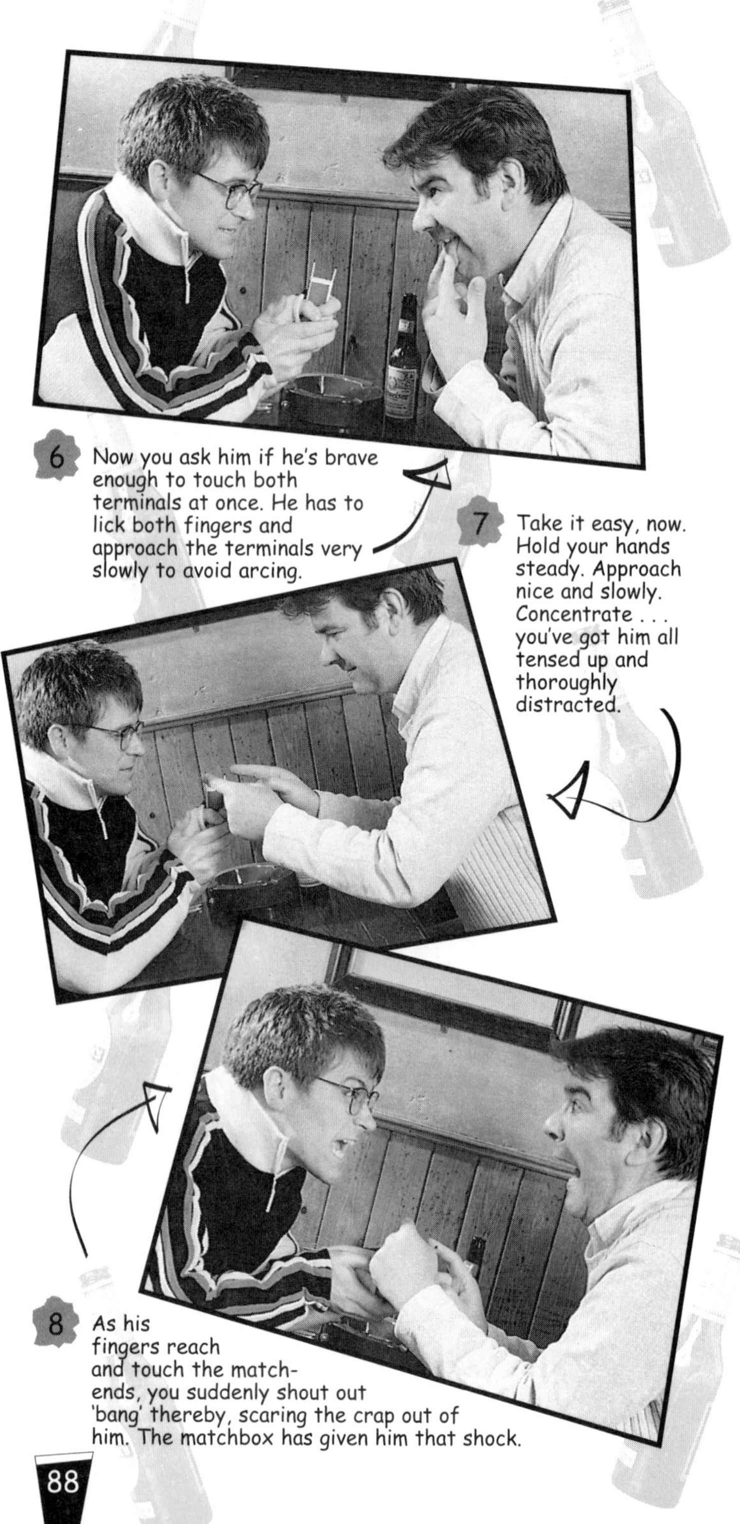

6 Now you ask him if he's brave enough to touch both terminals at once. He has to lick both fingers and approach the terminals very slowly to avoid arcing.

7 Take it easy, now. Hold your hands steady. Approach nice and slowly. Concentrate . . . you've got him all tensed up and thoroughly distracted.

8 As his fingers reach and touch the match-ends, you suddenly shout out 'bang' thereby, scaring the crap out of him. The matchbox has given him that shock.

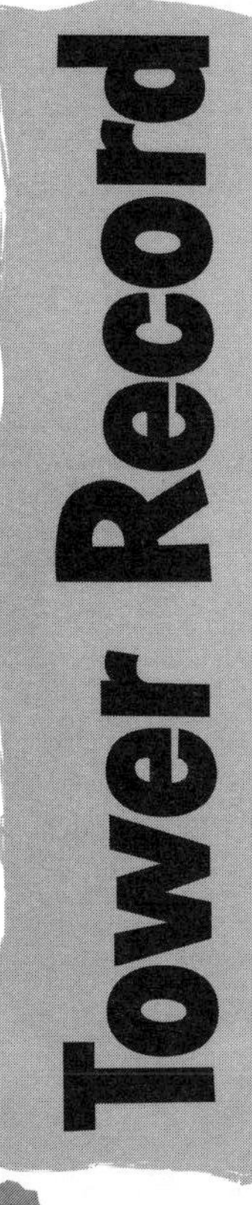

1 Here's an apparently simple challenge that could win you that cherry alcopop you've been longing for. Bet anyone they can't stack three ordinary half-pint glasses on top of one another on their outer rims.

2 It's just possible that they might make one glass stand on the rim of another, but when they try to add a third glass, the whole lot comes tumbling down.

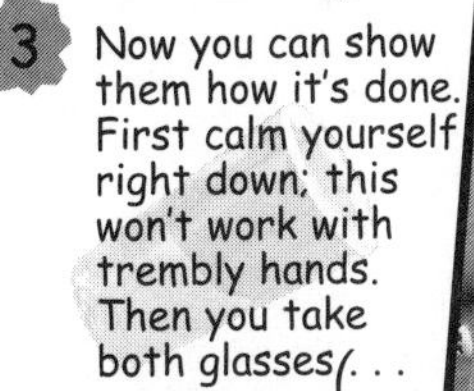

3 Now you can show them how it's done. First calm yourself right down; this won't work with trembly hands. Then you take both glasses . . .

4 Imagine the rim of the first glass is a clockface – put the second glass on top of its rim at about '10 o'clock'. Then place the third glass on top of the second at about '2 o'clock'.

5 Once you find just the right counterbalance point, the two glasses will sit there in a glass tower that looks like it should need a dozen tubes of superglue to hold it together. With a little practice, this is another sure-fire drink winner.

GIRLFRIEND IN A COMBER

1 If ever you doubted that there are strange invisible forces at work all around us, this is the trick to convince you, and any Doubting Thomases, or Celias or Juans*, amongst your mates. Take a match, balance it on the edge of a pound coin and cover it with a glass.

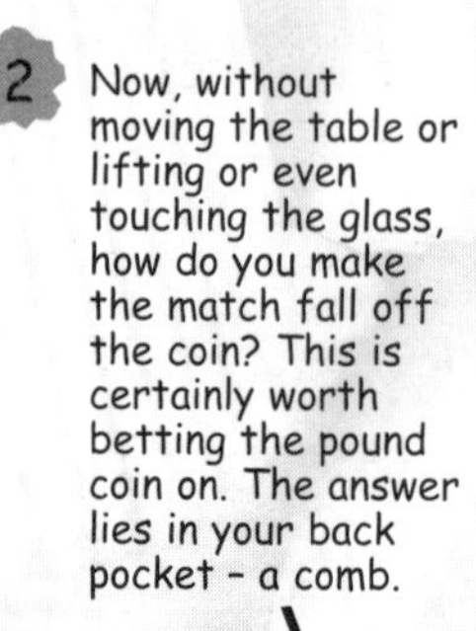

2 Now, without moving the table or lifting or even touching the glass, how do you make the match fall off the coin? This is certainly worth betting the pound coin on. The answer lies in your back pocket – a comb.

*I'm obviously hoping there might at least be some foreign sales of this book.

3 Rub the comb vigorously against your Barnet. If you're a slaphead, rub it against your jumper.

4 Now hold the statically charged comb close to the glass and move it back and forth – or forth and back if you're left handed. The static will cause the match to revolve slowly on the coin.

5 Gravity being what it is, the match will then fall off the coin. You've just won a pound. Don't spend it all at once.

Snap Happy

How do you mend a broken match in an instant so that it looks like new?

Can't be done?

Oh shut up.

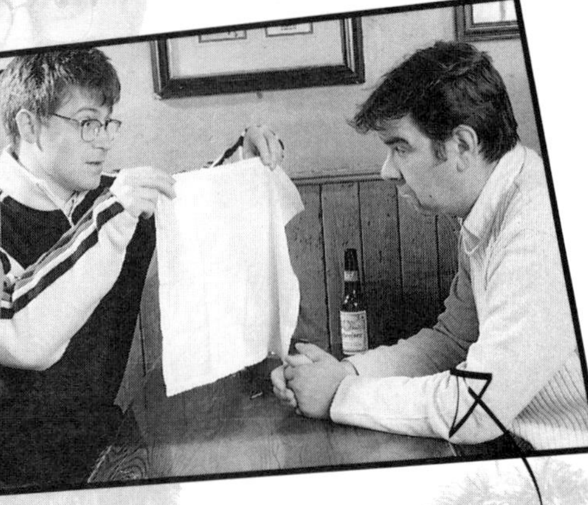

1 Show your drinking buddy a perfectly ordinary (preferably clean) handkerchief.

2 Hand him a wooden matchstick and ask him to place it in the middle of the hankie.

3 Wrap the matchstick up in the hankie and feel around until you find the wrapped match. Offer it to your friend.

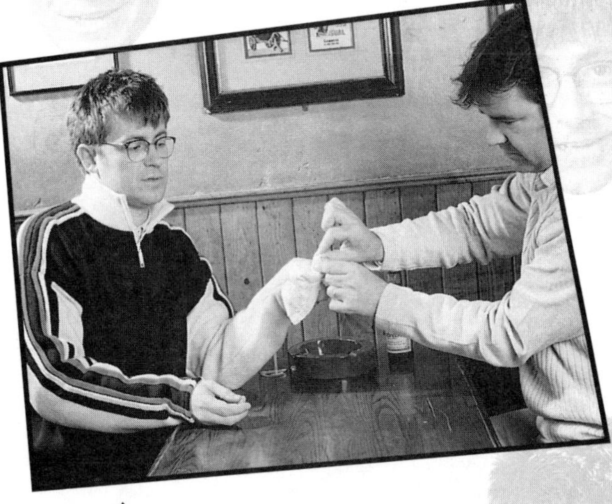

4 He must then use all of his mighty muscles to snap the match in two. Now you bet him a drink that you can make the match re-appear in pristine condition.

5 Once the drink's in the bag, unfurl the hankie with a flourish and a magic word. The match will fall to the table.

6 To his amazement, it will be unbroken. So how did you do it?

7 Well, a little preparation is required. First, find the little hole that lives at the corner seam of a hankie and feed a match into it.

8 Keep this covered with a finger when you show it to your victim, but offer it to him instead of the loose match when you ask him to snap the match. The match he placed in the hankie remains totally untouched.

There's No Catch

This is not a trick for anyone who suffers with back trouble and for anyone who doesn't, this can bring it on nicely.
If your willing volunteer likes kung fu fighting and has the reactions of a cat . . . tell him to sit down again.

1 The game is easy. You stand face to face. You are going to hold out a pen or pencil. Your friend will hold his hands, palms down, out a few inches above.

2 You are going to drop the pencil and he has to catch it before it hits the ground.

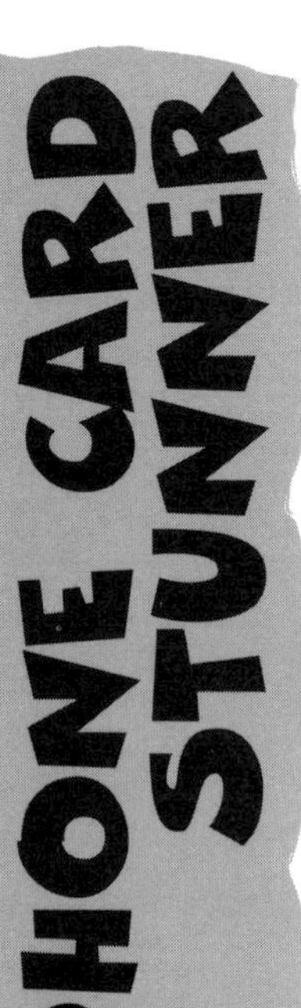

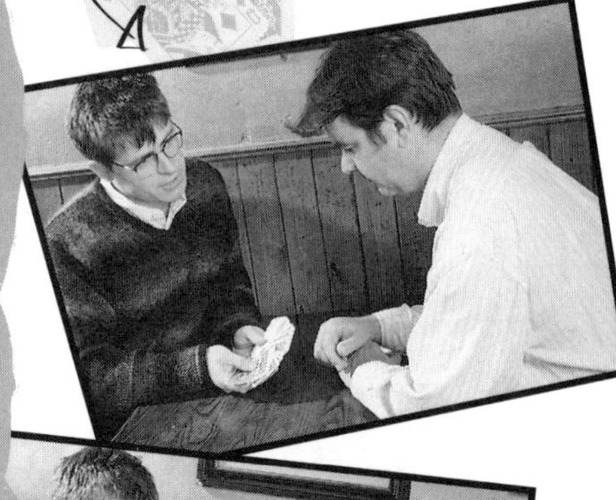

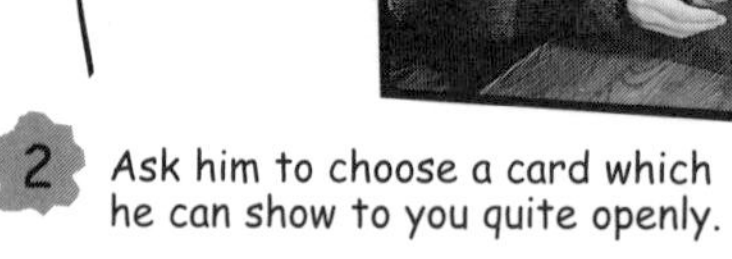

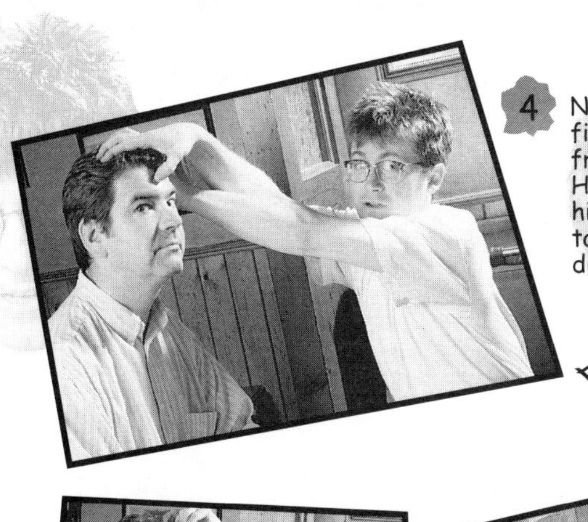

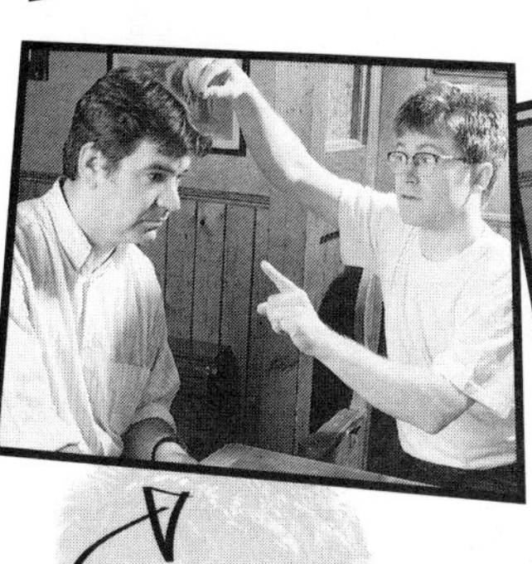

6 Make sure he sees the funny side when you tell him and don't let him bash his head on the table for too long, otherwise you might get your own head bashed in.

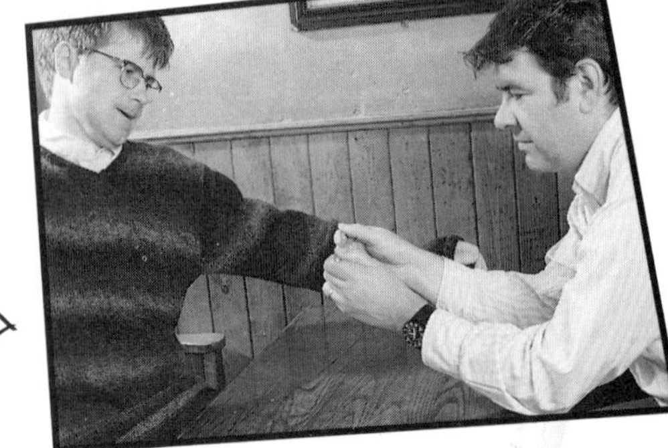

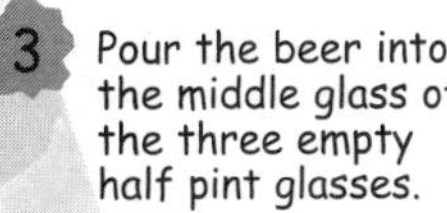

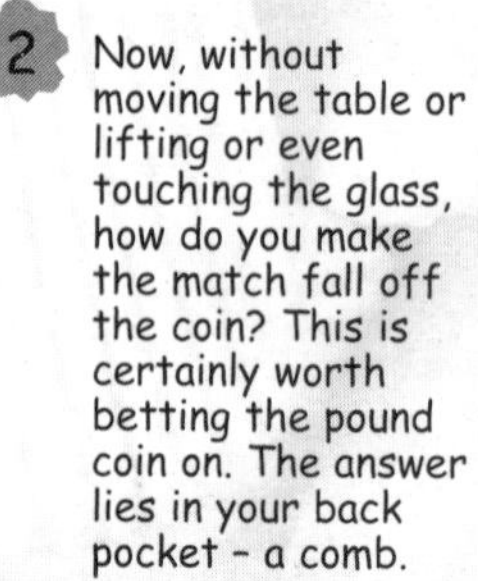

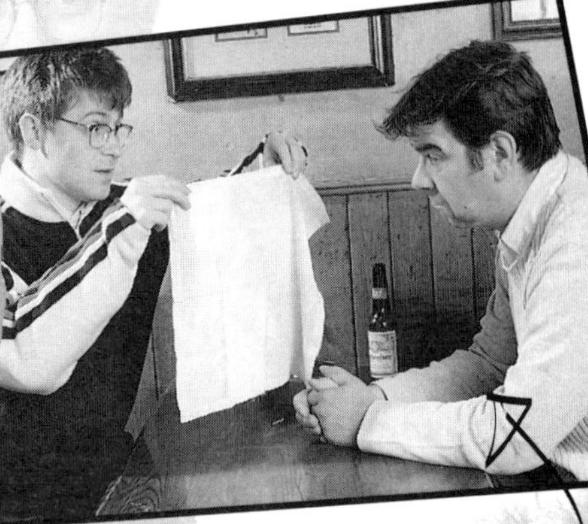

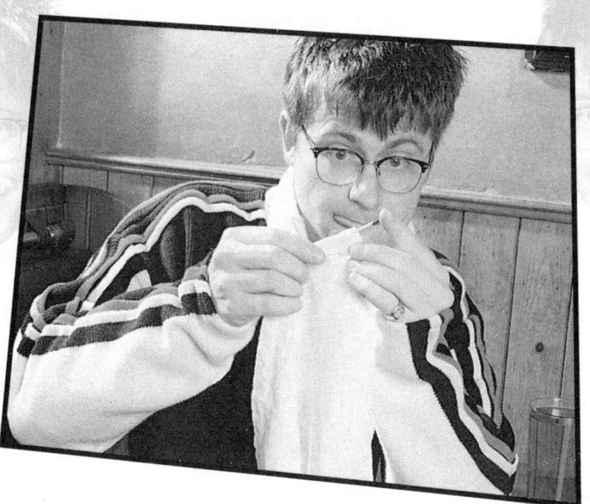

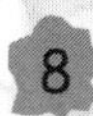